The Strange Case of Dr Jekyll and Mr Hyde

by Robert Louis Stevenson

Margaret Mulheran

Series Editors:
Sue Bennett and Dave Stockwin

HODDER
EDUCATION
AN HACHETTE UK COMPANY

The Publishers would like to thank the following for permission to reproduce copyright material.

Photo credits

p. 11 above Ingram, **below** TopFoto; **p. 13** Pictorial Press Ltd/Alamy; **p. 22** Mary Evans Picture Library/Alamy; **p. 24** The Print Collector/Alamy; **p. 26** IAM/akg-images; **p. 32** AF Archive/Alamy; **p. 42** AF Archive/Alamy; **p. 57** Photos 12/Alamy

Every effort has been made to trace all copyright holders, but if any have been inadvertently overlooked, the Publishers will be pleased to make the necessary arrangements at the first opportunity.

Although every effort has been made to ensure that website addresses are correct at time of going to press, Hodder Education cannot be held responsible for the content of any website mentioned in this book. It is sometimes possible to find a relocated web page by typing in the address of the home page for a website in the URL window of your browser.

Hachette UK's policy is to use papers that are natural, renewable and recyclable products and made from wood grown in sustainable forests. The logging and manufacturing processes are expected to conform to the environmental regulations of the country of origin.

Orders: please contact Bookpoint Ltd, 130 Park Drive, Milton Park, Abingdon, Oxon OX14 4SE. Telephone: (44) 01235 827720. Fax: (44) 01235 400454. Email education@bookpoint.co.uk Lines are open from 9 a.m. to 5 p.m., Monday to Saturday, with a 24-hour message answering service. You can also order through our website: www.hoddereducation.co.uk

ISBN: 978 1 4718 5368 5

© Margaret Mulheran, 2016

First published in 2016 by

Hodder Education,

An Hachette UK Company

Carmelite House

50 Victoria Embankment

London EC4Y 0DZ

www.hoddereducation.co.uk

Impression number   10 9 8 7 6 5 4 3 2 1

Year   2020 2019 2018 2017 2016

Cover photo: © phive2015/Thinkstock/iStock/Getty Images

Typeset in Bliss light 11/13pt by Integra Software Services Pvt. Ltd., Pondicherry, India

Printed in Italy

A catalogue record for this title is available from the British Library.

Contents

This guide is designed to help you to raise your achievement in your examination response to *The Strange Case of Dr Jekyll and Mr Hyde*. It is intended for you to use throughout your GCSE English literature course. It will help you when you are studying the novel for the first time and also during your revision.

The following features have been used throughout this guide to help you focus your understanding of the novel.

Target your thinking

A list of **introductory questions** labelled by Assessment Objective is provided at the beginning of each chapter to give you a breakdown of the material covered. They target your thinking in order to help you work more efficiently by focusing on the key messages.

Build critical skills

These boxes offer an opportunity to consider some **more challenging questions**. They are designed to encourage deeper thinking, analysis and exploratory thought. Building and practising critical skills in this way will give you a real advantage in the examination.

GRADE *FOCUS*

It is possible to know a novel well and yet still underachieve in the examination if you are unsure of what the examiners are looking for. The **GRADE FOCUS** boxes give a clear explanation of how you may be assessed, with an emphasis on the criteria for gaining a Grade 5 and a Grade 8.

REVIEW YOUR LEARNING

At the end of each chapter you will find the 'Review your learning' section to **test your knowledge**: a series of short, specific questions to ensure that you have understood and absorbed the key messages of the chapter. Answers to the 'Review your learning' questions are provided in the final section of the guide (page 100).

GRADE *BOOSTER*

Read and remember these pieces of helpful **grade-boosting advice**. They provide top tips from experienced teachers and examiners who can advise you on what to do, as well as what *not* to do, in order to maximise your chances of success in the examination.

Key quotation

Key quotations are highlighted for you, so that if you wish you may use them as **supporting evidence** in your examination answers. Further quotations, grouped by characterisation, key moments and theme, can be found in the 'Top ten' section on page 91 of the guide.

'*...that man is not truly one, but truly two*'

Introduction

Studying the text

You may find it useful to dip into this guide in sections as and when you need them, rather than reading it from start to finish. For example, the section on 'Context' can be read before you read the novel itself, since it offers an explanation of the relevant historical, cultural and literary background to the text. In 'Context' you will find information about aspects of Stevenson's life and times that influenced his writing; the particular issues with which Stevenson was concerned; and where the novel stands in terms of the literary tradition to which it belongs.

The relevant 'Plot and structure' sections in this guide could be helpful to you either before or after you read each chapter of *Dr Jekyll and Mr Hyde*. As well as a summary of events there is also commentary, so that you are aware of both key events and features in each chapter. Later, the sections on 'Characterisation', 'Themes' and 'Language, style and analysis' will help develop your thinking further, in preparation for written responses on particular aspects of the text.

Many students also enjoy the experience of being able to bring something extra to their classroom lessons in order to be 'a step ahead of the game'. Alternatively, you may have missed a classroom session or feel that you need a clearer explanation, and the guide can help you with this too.

An initial reading of the section on 'Assessment Objectives and skills' will enable you to make really effective notes in preparation for your written answers because you will have a very clear understanding of what examiners are looking for. The Assessment Objectives are what examination boards base their mark schemes on. In this section the AOs are broken down and clearly explained.

Revising the text

Whether you study the novel in a block of time close to the exam or much earlier in your GCSE English literature course, you will need to revise thoroughly if you are to achieve the very best grade that you can.

Reading this guide should, of course, never be a substitute for reading *Dr Jekyll and Mr Hyde*, but it can help. You should first remind yourself of what happens in the novel, and for this the chapter on 'Plot and structure' might be revisited in the first instance. You might then look at the 'Assessment Objectives and skills' section to ensure that you understand what the examiners are, in general, looking for.

'Tackling the exams' then gives you useful information on the exams and on question format, depending on which examination board specification you are following, as well as advice on the examination format and practical considerations such as the time available for the question and the Assessment Objectives that apply to it. Advice is also supplied on how to approach the question, writing a quick plan and 'working' with the text, since all of the examination boards use an extract-based question for *Dr Jekyll and Mr Hyde* (OCR also provides an additional, alternative discursive essay-type question). Focused advice on how you might improve your grade follows, and you need to read this section carefully.

You will find examples of exam-style responses in the 'Sample essays' section, with an examiner's comments in the margins so that you can see clearly how to move towards a Grade 5, and how then to move from a Grade 5 to a Grade 8.

All GCSE literature examinations are now 'closed book', meaning you may *not* take a copy of the text into the exam with you and you have to work from memory. The 'Top ten' quotations section should help you identify which key short quotations from *Dr Jekyll and Mr Hyde* to learn to support points about characterisation and themes, as well as being a revision aid to remind you which are the most important aspects of, and key moments in, the novel that you need to remember.

When writing about the novel, use this guide as a springboard to develop your own ideas. You should not read this guide in order to memorise chunks of it, ready to regurgitate in the exam. Examiners are not looking for set responses; identical answers are dull. They would like to see that you have used everything you have been taught – including by this guide – as a starting point for your own thinking. The examiners hope to reward you for perceptive thought, individual appreciation and varying interpretations. Try to show that you have engaged with the themes and ideas in the novel and that you have explored Stevenson's methods with an awareness of the context in which he wrote. Above all, don't be afraid to make it clear that you have enjoyed the novel.

There are, of course, a number of film versions of *Dr Jekyll and Mr Hyde*, but many of them deviate greatly from the original text. By all means watch them for fun; many will be thought-provoking, but remember that you are being examined on the text and that watching even the best films is no substitute for reading, or listening to, the original text several times. There are a number of audio versions out there. Some of them are free: it is worth exploring the possibilities using your favourite search engine! (See the next page or 'Wider reading', page 98.)

The most popular film adaptations include the following:

- 1920: silent film, starring John Barrymore
- 1941: starring Spencer Tracy and Ingrid Bergman
- 1968: starring Jack Palance; considered the most true to the text.

For audio versions, see:

- Lit2Go
- YouTube (offering many versions to choose from).

You might like to read some of Stevenson's other popular works:

- *Kidnapped*
- *Treasure Island*
- *A Child's Garden of Verse*
- *The Black Arrow*
- *Catriona*
- *The Master of Ballantrae*.

Enjoy referring to the guide as you study the text and good luck in your exam!

Target your thinking

- What is meant by 'context'? (**AO3**)
- How did Stevenson's life influence his work? (**AO3**)
- How did scientific advances and other literary works in the nineteenth century inform Stevenson's work? (**AO3**)
- What was London like in the time of Stevenson? (**AO3**)

What is context?

Knowledge of context will help you understand and appreciate your reading of *Dr Jekyll and Mr Hyde*, but what exactly *is* context?

> **GRADE BOOSTER**
>
> If you are entered for the Edexcel examination, AO3 is not assessed on the *Dr Jekyll and Mr Hyde* question. You might still like to read the material in this section, however, because it will increase your background knowledge and make your study of the text more meaningful.

Context is a wide-ranging term. It refers to the scientific advances and the historical and political circumstances of the time, as well as to the author's beliefs about those circumstances. It also refers to the way that more personal events in the author's own life may have influenced his or her thinking and writing. Finally, it may refer to **literary context**, and so it is important to be aware of developments in literature at the time.

Literary context: where the text stands in relation to its genre or how the writer might have been influenced by the work of other writers.

In the exam, part of the question will be extract-based and for this you are expected to be familiar with what has gone before and what comes after (particularly what comes *immediately* before and after) the events recorded in the passage. Remember, your purpose is primarily to interpret the text and to show how the text fits into the context. Make sure that your comments show how context relates to the text and use evidence from the text to support your viewpoint. Do not get side-tracked into giving a potted biography of Stevenson, or explaining historical events. Stick to the text and comment on how context might have influenced Stevenson's craft or viewpoint.

Romanticism: an artistic and literary movement in the eighteenth and nineteenth centuries that had an emphasis on emotions, particularly horror and terror. It contrasts with Classicism and Rationalism, which were based on reason, analysis and individualism.

The Strange Case of Dr Jekyll and Mr Hyde, or as it was called originally *Strange Case of Dr Jekyll and Mr Hyde*, was written by Robert Louis Stevenson in 1886 and is a fine example of Gothic literature (see page 14 below), which was popular in Victorian times. Publishers later changed the title to *The Strange Case of Dr Jekyll and Mr Hyde* to make it grammatically correct, but that was not Stevenson's original intention. This genre combines fiction with horror and **Romanticism** and, as the original title implies, there is also an element of the detective genre in this particular short novel or novella (meaning small novel).

Almost everyone in the English-speaking world has heard of 'Jekyll and Hyde', and the idea that the phrase represents a split personality – a struggle between good and evil inside the same person, or a person suffering from a severe personality disorder – has become the subject of films, TV series, musicals, comics and comedy sketches for over a century. The Robert Louis Stevenson webpage **http://robert-louis-stevenson.org** currently lists 134 films (of which 69 versions are considered very loose interpretations). *Dr Jekyll and Mr Hyde* is considered to be the most popular literary work adapted to film.

The original title *Strange Case of Dr Jekyll and Mr Hyde* has the ring of a crime novel or a detective story, rather like Conan Doyle's Sherlock Holmes stories, and if that were the case it appears to fall to Utterson to solve the mystery … except there is now no mystery. Most modern readers know the ending before they read the beginning. It is no longer a case to be solved but a story of horror, of terror and of the supernatural. Stevenson explores the idea of 'the duality of human nature' (see 'Themes', page 41) by creating a main character who can transform himself, initially at will, into his alter ego or other self, so he can indulge his bestial nature and commit, with impunity, random acts of violence, murder, and other unspecified crimes. This character doesn't even suffer from a guilty conscience when he changes back to Dr Jekyll. Jekyll sees himself as being completely innocent of the atrocities committed by Hyde, as he is not that person.

Despite a general familiarity with the dual personality or, as often misnamed, 'the split personality', most readers are only really familiar with the contents of the final chapter: 'Henry Jekyll's Full Statement of the Case'. Films concentrate on the transformation of Jekyll to Hyde in a spectacular science-fiction, sensationalist way. Stevenson does not present it this way. His is a story of horror and terror, the things dreams are made of: indeed the story came to him in a dream.

Robert Louis Stevenson's life (1850–94)

Robert Louis Stevenson was born in Edinburgh into a family of famous lighthouse engineers and, although his father would have liked him to follow the family tradition, because of his ill health he studied law instead. His family were devout **Presbyterians** and his nanny was believed to be very strictly religious. It is thought that when he grew up, Stevenson rejected their strict, sober ways and enjoyed a more **bohemian** style of living. He rejected Christianity and declared himself an atheist. He fell in love with a married American woman, Fanny Osbourne, who was ten years older, and married her when her divorce was finalised. At the time, this was considered quite scandalous.

Charles Dickens had written *A Christmas Carol* for the Christmas market in 1843 and Stevenson followed his example by timing the publication of *Dr Jekyll and Mr Hyde* in order to maximise sales. Gothic fiction was popular and a good money-spinner, and Stevenson suffered from ill health and was struggling to support his family. He remained financially dependent on his father well into his adult life and spent much of his life travelling to countries with warmer climates to alleviate the symptoms of a respiratory disease for which there was no known cure at the time.

▲ Robert Louis Stevenson

Presbyterian Church: a strict Protestant Christian sect that follows the teachings of John Calvin and adheres strictly to the Ten Commandments.

Bohemian: a nonconformist writer or artist who lives an unconventional lifestyle, which often scandalises people who uphold more traditional values regarding personal freedom, sex and family life.

▲ Service in St Giles's Church, Edinburgh

11

Strange Case of Dr Jekyll and Mr Hyde took Stevenson about ten weeks to write and it is thought to have been based on a dream he once had.

Many people believe that the story grew out of the conflict he felt from having grown up in a strictly religious family and the natural urges and the freedom he experienced later in his life. It is thought this may have caused him to question the relationship between the modern ideas of psychology and the religious values of his upbringing. The sales from the novella gave him financial independence from his father, which of course allowed him greater freedom and autonomy.

> **GRADE BOOSTER**
>
> It is helpful to have some knowledge of Stevenson's life as well as understanding the wider context of the novel, which may have affected the presentation of characters or themes. There is little to be gained, however, by simply 'bolting on' biographical or cultural details. They must always be related to the question you are answering.

Stevenson's London

The setting for *Dr Jekyll and Mr Hyde* is Victorian London, which was in many ways a very different place from the city we know today. Many people believe that Stevenson transposed his tale to London in order to gain wider appeal, but that he had his native Edinburgh in his mind. Dickens had already achieved great success by setting several of his novels in London, and Conan Doyle would go one step further by incorporating several real London venues into his Sherlock Holmes stories, published a year after *Dr Jekyll and Mr Hyde*. London clearly seems to have been a winning formula for literary success.

The nineteenth century was a time of huge social, scientific and technological change and with that change came an increase in crime and many social problems. It was the beginning of the Industrial Revolution, which transformed England from a mainly rural economy to an industrial one, with thousands of poor country-folk flocking to the cities in search of work. Foundries and factories were emerging on an unprecedented scale, and effluent and raw sewage were being pumped into the River Thames. Without an infrastructure to support them, many people were forced to live in unsanitary and overcrowded conditions.

▲ Slums in Victorian London

The alleys and courts of the city were dark and dirty; pollution gave rise to smoke and fog, often associated with crime and degeneracy. Stevenson uses Chapter 4 'The Carew Murder Case' in particular to raise awareness of this, when Utterson takes Inspector Newcomen to Hyde's house at nine in the morning:

> '...the fog lifted a little and showed him a dingy street, a gin palace, a low French eating-house ... and the next moment the fog settled down again on that part, as brown as umber and cut him off from his blackguardly surroundings.'

Night was seen as a time of lawlessness, mystery and fear. In *Dr Jekyll and Mr Hyde* light and dark are used very effectively to create atmosphere and reveal character. The two violent episodes – the trampling of the small girl and the murder of Danvers Carew – both take place either late at night or in the early hours of the morning, illuminated by either numerous street lamps (which would be much less bright and more yellow than we are used to today) or a full moon.

Build critical skills

How is night-time associated with crime and secrecy in the novella?

It appears that Utterson, Enfield and Poole have an inclination to walk around the streets of London in the middle of the night or take it upon themselves to visit Jekyll or Lanyon at this time. How might this add to the horror and terror of the novel?

13

The Gothic novel

The literary tradition of the Gothic novel began with Horace Walpole's novel *The Castle of Otranto*, written in 1764. Like Gothic films, the Gothic novel is written to frighten, thrill and terrify the reader, and there are numerous features or motifs that characterise a Gothic novel, although not every novel contains every feature.

This new genre became a tremendously popular source of entertainment as it caught the imagination of the educated reader at a time when science and industry were developing rapidly and social conditions were changing – causing people to question the role of religion in their lives as the ethics of work and wealth were shifting.

Common features of Gothic novels

- Set in a spooky castle or stately home built in a Gothic period or in the style of Gothic architecture and in a poor state of repair.
- Set in a house with a forbidden wing or secret passages.
- Involve a house whose owner is a sinister recluse.
- Include a crime or crimes as part of the story.
- Show a fascination with the past.
- Set in foreign parts.
- Involve weather which is often stormy, windy, dark and foggy or misty, with occasional sun, moonlight or artificial light for contrast.
- Explore strangely frightening and strangely familiar emotions, such as sexual desire, pleasure, power, pain (as in Bram Stoker's *Dracula*).
- Shock the readers out of their complacency and take them beyond their everyday experience.
- Open up the possibility of the existence of things beyond reason, such as through profound supernatural events.
- Address hidden emotions, fears or desires that might enslave a person.
- Contain monsters, controlling and menacing male figures, damsels in distress, pious virgins who are prone to fainting, other characters who are prone to fainting.
- Often have an unbelieving character who is eventually convinced of the supernatural.
- Explore conflicts between science, philosophy and accepted religious values.
- Morally uplifting – good always conquers evil.

Writers were by no means compelled to stick to a strict formula, and as the Gothic style developed these features seemed to evolve. The list is by no means exhaustive and writers like Stevenson developed their own individual style, including features they felt enhanced the thrill and excitement experienced by the reader. The overall effect of these features was for the reader to experience fear and horror through the suspension of disbelief, yet feel the comfort of a moral ending where good conquers evil, the righteous are rewarded and the wicked characters meet a sticky end. It is interesting to note at this point that none of the characters actually witnesses Jekyll's full transformation into Hyde, i.e. his descent into evil. Enfield and Utterson catch only a glimpse of this horror in 'The Incident at the Window'. Consider the effect the reverse transformation from Hyde into Jekyll had on Lanyon and you begin to understand the power of evil.

Build critical skills

When you have read the novel, decide which of these Gothic motifs have been addressed by Stevenson and explain how they have been addressed.

Possible interpretations of *Dr Jekyll and Mr Hyde*

All readers bring their own experience and ideas to whatever they read. Reading is not a passive activity: we can understand what we read only in the context of what our life experiences have been so far. We bring our own thoughts and feelings to whatever we read and these influence the effects a novel has on us. Many of us have a rich history of reading literary works, seeing films and watching dramas, whether at the cinema or on TV. We read newspapers and we are familiar with crime and punishment. We have formed our own ideas about justice, good and evil, and historical events. Many of us have experienced some kind of religion or we know people who have been influenced greatly by a religious faith. Imagine all these elements forming our personal lens, through which we study *Dr Jekyll and Mr Hyde*.

Context and Assessment Objectives (AOs)

When addressing the Assessment Objectives that relate to the context of the novel it is good to show you have interpreted Stevenson's work, but always be aware that there are many possible interpretations and yours is just one of those. To be taken seriously you must be able to justify your interpretation using sound reasoning and evidence from the text as a whole. This is rather like a detective fitting evidence together in order to develop an hypothesis. If any of the evidence doesn't fit, the detective has to go back to the drawing board. When satisfied that all the evidence has been taken into account, he or she forms a theory that must be tested before any firm conclusions are drawn. It is wise to keep an open mind about what Stevenson intended and always to frame your answers as *possible* interpretations. You cannot draw any definitive conclusions. It is particularly important not to draw any conclusions relating to the autobiographical nature of the novel, although it is perfectly acceptable to draw parallels with possible beliefs and events of the time.

Stevenson's work is a *classic*, which means it has a lasting relevance way beyond its time and makes sense even when new scientific discoveries and technological advances have been made.

Victorian society

Many novelists have written about the nature of Victorian society as exemplified in history books. The workhouse was in existence; crime was rife, particularly in the growing cities; there was a big gap between the rich and the poor. Established religion was powerful. Respectable people went to church and performed charitable works. There was a notion of the 'deserving' poor and the 'undeserving' poor. The former endured hardship without complaint and showed excessive gratitude for any crumb thrown to them from the rich man's table; the latter were thieves and vagabonds who were not content to go hungry and reap their reward in heaven. It was all to do with respectability (see 'Themes', page 46). Sobriety, restraint, prudence, thrift, modesty and chastity were the virtues held up for people – especially poor people – to aspire to. There was an underlying belief that rich people were rich because they deserved to be and that was what God wanted, and that the converse was true also. There was also a tradition of philanthropy, of rich men setting up charities to help the deserving poor. These included William Booth, the founder of the Salvation Army, and the Cadbury family in Bourneville, who were famous for looking after their workers. Such charities did their best to reach the most needy, but they could not change the lives of the majority.

Many rich people paid lip service to Victorian virtues, but this was a veneer designed by the Victorians to make them seem caring. The reality was different. Poor people were hanged for petty theft. Women were the property of their husbands or fathers – if they were lucky enough to have a protector; otherwise they could be exploited in every way by their masters. Only male property owners were allowed to vote, so women and working-class men had no power. Many men, women and children survived by prostitution. Male homosexuality was illegal; female homosexuality was believed not to exist. The fact that male homosexuality was illegal gave rise to it being termed 'the blackmailer's charter'. Interestingly, both Utterson and Enfield believe that Jekyll is being blackmailed by Hyde!

This is the historical context of *Dr Jekyll and Mr Hyde* and so it is easy to see how the novel could be seen as a critique of a male-dominated society, where successful men were outwardly charitable and concerned for the less fortunate but committed shady acts under the cover of darkness. This is implicit throughout the novel but none of these acts is made explicit, though we are told that certainly Jekyll – even before he became Hyde – did things he might be ashamed of in his youth, as did the ultra-respectable Utterson. The concept of the duality of human nature and the duality of society lends itself beautifully to Victorian times.

What could the shameful acts committed by Jekyll and Utterson include? Indulging excessively in alcohol or drugs? Gambling? Visiting mistresses or prostitutes? Pursuing (then-illegal) homosexual relationships? There are many possibilities. (They are just possibilities! Under no circumstances are you to come to a definite conclusion regarding the sexual orientation of the characters, but it is acceptable to point out that they were unmarried and attended men-only social evenings.)

The lifestyle of Stevenson's characters is very individual. The main characters are all middle-class, unmarried men. They are all mature. Most of them have a tendency to walk the streets late at night and in the early hours of the morning, whether on business or seeking pleasure is not stipulated. None of the women in the novel is named and all but the small girl are servants.

Clearly Jekyll is experimenting with psychotic drugs such as laudanum (which was *not* illegal), and this forms the basis of the story. The taking of laudanum was widespread in Victorian times, both as pain relief and as a recreational drug. Laudanum was a solution of opium drugs (modern forms of which are heroin, morphine and codeine) in alcohol.

Could an interpretation be that the novel is a warning about the dangers of drug-taking and its possible side effects? This clearly fits a modern context, as research suggests that taking certain illegal drugs may contribute to psychosis (mental illness) in some people. British society did not become unduly alarmed about recreational drug use until the 1960s, however, when it spread into youth culture. A more likely interpretation in Victorian times would be that the novel serves as warning about the dangers of science and scientific research running out of control.

It is easy to visualise Stevenson's fascination with the activities of such an underworld, having been brought up within such a restrictive environment, and once he had cast off his religious upbringing and declared himself an atheist, there was a whole 'other' world for him to explore in his writing and possibly in his private life, though there is no evidence in the text to support the notion that it is autobiographical in any way.

GRADE BOOSTER

Be careful about drawing definite conclusions, but by all means stick to the facts and present these ideas as possibilities in your exam responses.

GRADE *FOCUS*

Grade 5

To achieve a Grade 5, students need to show a clear understanding of the context in which the novel was written.

Grade 8

To achieve a Grade 8, students need to make perceptive, critical comments about the ways that contextual factors affect the choices Stevenson makes.

REVIEW YOUR LEARNING

(Answers are given on p. 100.)

1 What stopped Stevenson from following his chosen profession?

2 What is meant by the term 'context'?

3 What was the greatest change that the publication of *Dr Jekyll and Mr Hyde* made to Stevenson's life?

4 How might the ideas in Stevenson's novel be relevant to society today?

5 Why do you think Stevenson chose to set *Dr Jekyll and Mr Hyde* in London?

6 What are the differences between a Presbyterian and a bohemian lifestyle?

7 What do you understand by the term 'Gothic'?

8 What was laudanum?

9 Name two aspects of Stevenson's upbringing that he rejected as an adult.

10 What important piece of advice have you been given in this chapter about addressing context in your essays?

Target your thinking

- What are the main events of the novel? (**AO1**)
- How do these events unfold chapter by chapter? (**AO1**, **AO2**)
- How does Stevenson structure these events? (**AO2**)

Structure

Stevenson separates the novel into ten chapters, each with its own heading. Although they are not numbered in the Penguin Modern Classics edition, it would be helpful to pencil in the chapter numbers for ease of reference. The first eight chapters of the narrative are written in the third person, almost entirely from the viewpoint of Utterson, the lawyer – after which the storyline is complete. The action in the novel takes place in London over a period of 17 months, some time in the mid-nineteenth century.

> **GRADE BOOSTER**
>
> Usually, the examination question will explain briefly where in the novel the extract is taken from. It won't necessarily tell you what happens just before or just after the extract. When you are writing about plot and structure, however, it is helpful if you do know the sequence of events. You need to know the novel well and this can only be achieved by reading it (or listening to it) several times.

Chapters 9 and 10 do not add to the plot but attempt to give meaning to what Utterson has witnessed. Chapter 9 is written in the first person, in the voice of Dr Lanyon, and Chapter 10 takes the form of a statement from Dr Jekyll, written immediately prior to his death. These two chapters reveal the true nature of the secrets of Henry Jekyll and Lanyon's reluctance to acknowledge the validity of Jekyll's 'scientific' experiments. Stevenson brings together all the threads of his story to reach a **denouement**.

Denouement: the final outcome when all the complex events of the novel fit together and a conclusion is reached.

The denouement of *Dr Jekyll and Mr Hyde* does not take into account any events after Hyde's death, and Stevenson leaves his readers to ponder what Utterson's next moves might be. The fact that there is not a clear resolution only adds to the thrill and the terror experienced by the reader.

The first eight chapters of the novel follow a chronological timeline, as outlined in the table below.

Chapter	Timing	What happens
1 'The Story of the Door'	One Sunday afternoon in November 18–	Utterson and Enfield are taking their regular Sunday walk when Enfield narrates a shocking episode that he had witnessed in the vicinity: a child being trampled.
2 'The Search for Mr Hyde'	The same evening	Utterson returns home and examines the will of his friend Dr Jekyll.
3 'Dr Jekyll Was Quite at Ease'	Two weeks later	Dr Jekyll holds a small dinner party and Utterson brings up the topic of Jekyll's will.
4 'The Carew Murder Case'	Nearly a year later, October 18–(+1), at 11 p.m.	Sir Danvers Carew, a Conservative Member of Parliament, is beaten and trampled to death.
	The next day at 8 a.m.	Utterson identifies the body.
	The same day at 9 a.m.	Utterson takes the police to Hyde's rooms in a house in Soho.
5 'The Incident of the Letter'	The same day, late in the afternoon	Jekyll gives Utterson a letter from Hyde.
6 'The Remarkable Incident of Dr Lanyon'	For more than two months afterwards	Jekyll is at peace.
	8th January 18–(+2)	Utterson, Lanyon and others dine at Jekyll's house. It is just like the old days.
	12th, 14th, 15th January 18–(+2)	Utterson tries to see Jekyll but is not admitted.
	16th January 18–(+2)	Utterson dines with an unnamed guest.
	17th January 18–(+2)	Utterson visits Lanyon, who appears to be dying.
	18th January 18–(+2)	Utterson sends a letter to Jekyll informing him of Lanyon's ill health. He receives a reply the same day, confirming that the rift between Jekyll and Lanyon is irreparable.
	25th January 18–(+2)	Lanyon takes to his bed.
	First week in February 18–(+2)	Lanyon dies.
	Later in February 18–(+2)	The night after Lanyon's funeral, Utterson receives a package containing a sealed letter, written by Lanyon before his death, with the instruction that it is not to be opened until after the death or disappearance of Jekyll.
7 'The Incident at the Window'	On a Sunday a few weeks later	On one of their regular walks, Utterson and Enfield see Jekyll sitting by the open window of his cabinet, taking the air.
8 'The Last Night'	'A wild, cold, seasonable night in March' 18–(+2)	Utterson and Poole break down the door to Jekyll's cabinet and find the body of Hyde.

The final two chapters cover the same time period as those in chapters 1 to 8. Chapter 9, 'Dr Lanyon's Narrative', gives the contents of the sealed letter delivered to Utterson in Chapter 6 and written shortly before Lanyon's death in February 18–(+2). It covers the events shown below. Note that there is an inconsistency concerning the timing: in the text Jekyll's letter to Lanyon is dated 10th December 18–. The reader must assume that this was an error which occurred in the editing process. It occurs in all the editions of the text. The letter had to be written after the dinner party on 8th January 18–(+2).

Chapter	Timing	What happens
9 'Dr Lanyon's Narrative'	9th January 18–(+2)	Lanyon receives a letter from Jekyll with instructions to obtain chemicals from his cabinet and to be ready to receive a visitor after midnight.
	14th January 18–(+2)	Soon after midnight, after taking a concoction of the chemicals, Hyde (the expected visitor) metamorphoses into Henry Jekyll in front of Lanyon, who is so deeply shocked he dies a few weeks later.

Chapter 10, 'Henry Jekyll's Full Statement of the Case', then presents Jekyll's account of events, written just before the death of Jekyll/Hyde in March 18–(+2).

Plot

The following chapter summaries provide a brief account of the content of each chapter.

Chapter 1 'The Story of the Door'

The novel opens with a detailed character description of Gabriel John Utterson, from whose perspective 80 per cent of the novel is written.

Key quotation

Utterson appears to be a very dull, uninspiring character. He clings to rational explanations wherever possible: 'A man of rugged countenance, that was never lighted by a smile; cold, scanty and embarrassed in discourse; backward in sentiment; lean, long, dusty, dreary, and yet somehow lovable.'

On one of their regular Sunday afternoon walks, Utterson and his distant relative Richard Enfield pass through a busy commercial street in London. Enfield points out a door that is connected to a very strange incident he witnessed in the early hours of the morning a few weeks earlier. A particularly small, ugly man had collided with a young girl, knocking her over. The man then proceeded to trample over her, leaving her screaming with pain and shock, before attempting to flee. The perpetrator turns out to be Edward Hyde, who is forced by Enfield, a passing doctor and the girl's family to pay compensation of £100. Hyde uses a key to enter through the door and returns with cash and a cheque signed by a third party.

Unknown to Enfield (and the reader at this point), Utterson recognises the door as being the back entrance to the grand residence and work premises of a close friend. He does not reveal the name of the friend and due to a mutual distaste for gossip, he and Enfield agree not to discuss this matter again.

This chapter is important for its description of Hyde. Once Hyde's name is mentioned, Utterson knows that it was the door to Jekyll's laboratory and that the cheque was signed by Jekyll.

As you read through the novel, notice how Stevenson adds to Hyde's description through the eyes of other characters. It is interesting that Enfield immediately jumps to the conclusion that Hyde is blackmailing the person who wrote the cheque.

Chapter 2 'The Search for Mr Hyde'

The same evening, Utterson returns home and examines the will of his friend Dr Jekyll. It states that in the event of Jekyll's death or disappearance for a period of more than three months, his 'friend and benefactor Edward Hyde' would inherit all his wealth and possessions. Utterson had previously strenuously advised against this action and, although he had the will in his possession for safe-keeping, refused to have any part in drawing it up.

Utterson is alarmed and decides to visit Dr Lanyon, a mutual friend of both himself and Jekyll. Lanyon knows nothing about Hyde and has little interest in Jekyll following a serious professional disagreement.

Utterson returns home and has disturbing dreams involving Hyde. Being a practical man, Utterson is alarmed after encountering a man with no face in his dream, and when he wakes he goes in search of Hyde. He accosts him late one night at the door of the rear entrance of Jekyll's premises. He is surprised when Hyde gives him his Soho address and shows his face clearly. This encounter fills Utterson with 'unknown disgust, loathing and fear'.

Utterson later visits Jekyll, who is not at home. Poole explains that Mr Hyde is a regular visitor who spends most of his time in the old dissecting rooms, and that Jekyll has told the servants that they must obey Hyde's orders.

▲ Mr Hyde on a late night excursion

Again the atmosphere of secrecy is developed: the will is securely hidden; Lanyon loses his temper when he refers to Jekyll. The reader is not told the details of the dispute between Jekyll and Lanyon. The reader is intended to be intrigued by shameful wrongs in Utterson's past, the details of which are never divulged.

The setting – both the atmosphere created in the dream and in the city at night when Utterson lies in wait for Hyde – is important. Utterson's description of Hyde gives the reader a clearer picture of his repulsiveness. Utterson reaches the same conclusion as Enfield, which is that Hyde is blackmailing Jekyll. Surprisingly for such a dour character, the reader learns that Utterson has done things in the past that he is careful to hide.

Chapter 3 'Dr Jekyll Was Quite at Ease'

Two weeks later Dr Jekyll holds a small dinner party and, after the other guests have departed, Utterson broaches the subject of Jekyll's will.

Build critical skills

Make a note of the initial description of Jekyll in this chapter in order to compare it to the description of Jekyll in Chapter 5 'The Incident of the Letter'.

This is the first time the reader meets Henry Jekyll, who appears to be very fond of Utterson. Jekyll is aware of both Utterson's and Lanyon's disapproval of the contents of the will but extracts a reluctant promise that, if necessary, Utterson will execute it according to his wishes. His wishes are that Hyde will be his heir and the main beneficiary. He demands absolute secrecy. Utterson learns that the rift between Jekyll and Lanyon is based on a profound disagreement over science, which Jekyll treats in a light-hearted way. Jekyll assures Utterson that his concern is appreciated but not needed.

Chapter 4 'The Carew Murder Case'

Sir Danvers Carew, a Conservative Member of Parliament, is beaten and trampled to death late at night. The brutal murder is witnessed by a maid from her bedroom window overlooking the street. She recognises the killer as Edward Hyde.

The police find a letter on the body addressed to Mr Utterson and, when he is called to identify the body, he recognises the broken murder weapon as having been part of a walking stick he had given to Jekyll as a gift.

Utterson takes the police to Hyde's house in Soho, where they meet only the housekeeper. There is a detailed description of Soho given here, which might be useful to refer to if answering a question on setting.

Key quotation

'Mr Hyde was pale and dwarfish: he gave the impression of deformity without any nameable malformation, he had a displeasing smile.'

Build critical skills

Why do you think Stevenson includes a dream sequence for Utterson? What effect is this meant to have on the reader?

Key quotation

'the moment I choose, I can be rid of Mr Hyde.'

Key quotation

'This is a private matter, and I beg you to let it sleep'

Build critical skills

Notice once again that the two men, Hyde and Danvers Carew, are out conducting their business at night. What could Carew possibly have said to provoke such a violent reaction in Hyde?

Build critical skills

Make a note of all the references to Hyde looking like some kind of beast in Chapters 4, 8 and 9. What is the effect of these on the reader?

During their search of the house, Utterson and the police find the ashes of piles of papers and the charred remains of a chequebook, together with the other half of the broken murder weapon. Once again it is difficult to gain a reliable physical description of Hyde, even from people who have met him on several occasions.

This chapter describes in great detail the horrific, violent attack on Carew and would have greatly shocked Victorian readers. There are several examples of the usage of language to depict terror and horror and other elements commonly included in the Gothic novel.

Chapter 5 'The Incident of the Letter'

Utterson visits Jekyll in his laboratory and observes a profound change in him. He was 'looking deadly sick'. Utterson has come to help his friend but wants assurance that Jekyll is not hiding the fugitive, Hyde.

Key quotation

Jekyll: 'I am quite done with him [Hyde]. I was thinking of my own character, which this hateful business had rather exposed.'

Jekyll shows Utterson a letter, allegedly from Hyde, in which he apologises for his behaviour and states that he will not bother Jekyll again. Utterson asks to see the envelope. Jekyll says that he accidentally destroyed it but that it had been delivered by hand. On his departure, Utterson asks Poole to confirm this, but the butler is sure that the only deliveries on that day had been by post.

Key quotation

Note the change in tone as well as content in Jekyll's reference to Hyde: 'I swear to God I will never set eyes on him again.'

On Utterson's return home he shows the letter to his head clerk, Mr Guest, who is a handwriting expert. He remarks on the similarity of the handwriting to Jekyll's, although it slants in the opposite direction. Utterson is left wondering why Jekyll should forge a letter for a murderer.

The reader can visualise the workrooms at the end of Jekyll's garden from the detailed description of the laboratories, the dissecting rooms and his cabinet. This is an important chapter regarding setting and atmosphere. The fog, the dim light, the barred windows, Jekyll's cold hands and feverish manner – all add to the atmosphere of fear, secrecy and foreboding. Once more the idea of secrecy is developed when Utterson locks the letter in his safe and demands silence on the matter from Guest. The reader is left to ponder how Utterson will rationalise this twist in events.

▲ Utterson: '"What!" he thought. "Henry Jekyll forge for a murderer!"'

Build critical skills

Look back at the note you made about Jekyll in response to 'Build critical skills' on page 23. Comment on how Stevenson is slowly revealing the character of Henry Jekyll and showing two sides to his character.

Chapter 6 'The Remarkable Incident of Dr Lanyon'

In the next few months much of Hyde's wicked behaviour comes to light but, despite a substantial reward being offered, he has disappeared completely. Following the disappearance of Hyde, Jekyll briefly returns to his old self and resumes his practice of holding dinner parties for his friends, including Utterson and Lanyon. Four days after his last dinner party, held on 8th January, however, Jekyll begins to refuse visitors. At the same time, Lanyon takes ill and goes into terminal decline. After several failed attempts to see Jekyll, on 17th January Utterson visits Lanyon and is shocked to see 'He had his death warrant written legibly on his face.'

When Utterson remarks that Jekyll is ill also, Lanyon firmly states that he wants no more to do with Jekyll and, unless he agrees to avoid 'the cursed topic', Utterson must leave. He apologises to Utterson and gives him a package containing two envelopes, saying the reasons will become clear after his death.

Utterson writes to Jekyll informing him of Lanyon's condition and is surprised when Jekyll in his reply agrees that neither of them should ever meet with Jekyll again and admits that he is entirely to blame for the rift between himself and Lanyon.

Three weeks later Lanyon dies. Utterson is reminded of Jekyll's will and his strange legacy to Edward Hyde when he reads on an envelope addressed to himself from Lanyon: 'Not to be opened until the death or disappearance of Dr Henry Jekyll.' Utterson feels obliged to honour Lanyon's wishes regarding not opening the envelope. Instead he goes to visit Jekyll but is, again, refused admittance.

GRADE BOOSTER

```
You should remind yourself here that Hyde is the
other side of Jekyll's character and this side of the
character is still within Jekyll, thus illustrating
the duality within man. Students aiming for the highest
levels need to understand Jekyll's false thinking at
the beginning of Chapter 10, where he explains how
initially the results of his experiment provided the
ideal solution to his problem.
```

Build critical skills

Note Utterson's change in attitude towards Jekyll at the end of this chapter. What do you think it is that Utterson is struggling with?

Key quotation

'*Much of his past was unearthed, indeed, and all disreputable: tales came out of the man's cruelty, at once so callous and violent, of his vile life, of his strange associates...*'

Build critical skills

In Chapter 10, Jekyll attempts to distance himself from the actions of Hyde. Ultimately, the truth is revealed – that he is Hyde as much as he is Jekyll, and in the end he is unable to suppress the profane side of his character. What might Stevenson be implying about the nature of evil?

Chapter 7 'The Incident at the Window'

On the Sunday, Utterson and Enfield are taking their usual walk when they see Jekyll's door, which reminds them of Hyde and the terrible events that had taken place. Enfield confesses to feeling foolish for not realising they had been at the back of Jekyll's residence when he told Utterson about the girl being trampled.

They step into the courtyard and notice Jekyll sitting beside an open window taking the air. Although very miserable initially and looking forward to the end of his suffering, Jekyll is pleased to see his old friend and agrees to stay and talk. Suddenly, though, a look of 'abject terror and despair' crosses his face and he slams the window shut, but not before Utterson and Enfield are visibly shaken to their roots. Enfield and Utterson glimpse Jekyll spontaneously metamorphose into Hyde before he violently closes the window of his laboratory.

Utterson appeals to God and they return home in deep shock. They do not discuss what they have seen. (This foreshadows events that are explained in 'Dr Lanyon's Narrative', Chapter 9.)

▲ Jekyll with a look of 'abject terror and despair'

Build critical skills

The reader is left wondering how Utterson will attempt to rationalise this latest event. Will he come to the same conclusion as Lanyon?

Key quotation

'They were both pale and there was an answering horror in their eyes.'

Build critical skills

How does the change in Poole's appearance when he arrives resemble that of Lanyon in Chapter 6?

Chapter 8 'The Last Night'

Poole arrives one evening, begging Utterson to accompany him to Jekyll's laboratory as he suspects Jekyll has been murdered. Jekyll's servants are gathered together for safety in the hall and are terrified. From outside the door, Poole and Utterson speak to the person inside the cabinet. A voice, which they do not identify as Jekyll's, refuses them entry. Poole believes that this creature killed Jekyll eight days previously when he heard Jekyll '...cry out upon the name of God'. Since that time the only communications Poole has received have been frantic written requests for him to obtain a drug, and later instructions to return it because it was not pure and to order it from a different firm.

Utterson is shocked when Poole admits that he had seen the occupant of the room when the latter had slipped out of the cabinet to search the theatre for the drug. He was adamant it was not Jekyll. Eventually Poole admits to believing it was Hyde. Despite the pleading from within the cabinet from the voice, now clearly identifiable as Hyde's, Poole breaks down the door with an axe.

Utterson and Poole discover the twitching body of Hyde, who has clearly drunk poison. They proceed to look for the body of Jekyll but find only a large envelope containing Jekyll's updated will (where Utterson's name replaces that of Hyde as Jekyll's sole beneficiary), together with other documents.

Utterson goes home to read the two documents, 'Dr Lanyon's Narrative' and 'Henry Jekyll's Full Statement of the Case' (which make up Chapters 9 and 10), promising to return by midnight when they will send for the police.

This chapter concludes the third person narrative from the perspective of Gabriel Utterson.

Chapter 9 'Dr Lanyon's Narrative'

There are no new events in this chapter. These events would fit into the chronology of events in Chapter 6 'The Remarkable Incident of Dr Lanyon'.

Lanyon gives an account of how Jekyll makes a mysterious request for his help in obtaining a specific drawer and its contents from his cabinet, and bringing it back to his own consulting rooms.

Hyde arrives at midnight and mixes a cocktail of the substances contained in the drawer. He offers to leave with the substance or to drink it in Lanyon's presence. Lanyon chooses the latter and observes Hyde transform into Jekyll.

Lanyon is shocked to his core and his health is so badly affected that he fears he has little time left to live. He learns the true nature of Jekyll's experiments, which he finds terrifying and shocking. Lanyon also learns much about human nature: Jekyll is seeking revenge here for Lanyon's earlier dismissal of his scientific research and Lanyon's 'greed of curiosity' gets the better of him.

Chapter 10 'Henry Jekyll's Full Statement of the Case'

There are no new events in this chapter. This statement is written just before Jekyll/Hyde takes his own life, and all the events in the previous chapters are put into context.

Jekyll was born into a privileged background; he was affluent and successful in his chosen profession and admired by his peers. He also lived a secret life in which he indulged his pleasures and was to an extent ashamed of his activities. The nature of these activities is not revealed.

Key quotation

'Sir, if that was my master, why did he have a mask upon his face?'

Key quotation

Hyde tempting Lanyon to stay and watch the transformation: '…a new province of knowledge and new avenues to fame and power shall be laid open to you…'

Build critical skills

Robert Louis Stevenson would have had a very extensive knowledge of the Old Testament. According to the serpent, why did God forbid Adam and Eve to eat an apple from the Tree of Knowledge?

Jekyll concludes that a person has more than one side to his personality and that he had proceeded to explore this idea through scientific research. He discovered a drug that brought about a painful metamorphosis from the respectable person of Dr Jekyll into the depraved Mr Hyde, and for a time he enjoyed living a secret double life about which he felt no shame.

Jekyll maintains that he was not a hypocrite, but the reader may doubt this. He took no responsibility for the actions of Hyde when he emerged again as Jekyll. Hyde was a psychopathic character who felt no responsibility for the pain he caused others.

Gradually the Hyde or evil side of his nature began to take over and Jekyll could no longer control his transformations by the use of drugs. After the murder of Carew, and after revealing the duality of his nature to Lanyon, Jekyll realised he was doomed. He kills himself before his metamorphosis into the evil character of Hyde is completely irreversible; it is Hyde's body, however, that is found by Poole and Utterson.

Build critical skills

Consider why, although it was Jekyll who killed himself, it was Hyde's body that remained. What point might Stevenson be making?

Key quotation

'I was in no sense a hypocrite; both sides of me were in dead earnest; I was no more myself when I laid aside restraint and plunged into shame, than when I laboured in the eye of day, at the furtherance of knowledge or the relief of sorrow and suffering.'

Build critical skills

What was Stevenson able to achieve by including the testimonies of Lanyon and Jekyll at the end of the novel instead of continuing the narrative in a straightforward chronological way?

GRADE *FOCUS*

Grade 5

To achieve a Grade 5, students must show a clear and detailed understanding of the whole text and the effects created by its structure.

Grade 8

To achieve a Grade 8, students' responses will display a comprehensive understanding of implicit and explicit meanings in the text as a whole and will examine and evaluate in detail the writer's use of structure.

REVIEW YOUR LEARNING

(Answers are given on p. 100.)

1 Why do Utterson and Enfield suspect Jekyll is being blackmailed?

2 Who is 'about as emotional as a bagpipe'?

3 How does Utterson's dream relate to reality?

4 What are the stipulations made in Jekyll's original will?

5 Who calls whom 'an ignorant, blatant pedant', and why?

6 Copy down the piece of text that describes the old woman at Hyde's rooms in Soho and comment on her behaviour.

7 Why do you think Lanyon dies?

8 Why is Poole convinced that Jekyll has been murdered by Hyde?

9 Who says 'If I am the chief of the sinners, I am chief of the sufferers too'? What do you think he means?

10 Why do you think Lanyon agreed to carry out Jekyll's request?

Target your thinking

- Who's who in *Dr Jekyll and Mr Hyde*? (**AO1**)
- What is the difference between character and characterisation? (**AO2**)
- How does Stevenson present the characters? (**AO1**, **AO2**, **AO3**)

Who's who in *Dr Jekyll and Mr Hyde*?

GRADE *BOOSTER*

To gain higher marks it is useful to show you understand that the characters are all constructs, not real people. They have been created by the author to fulfil his purpose in writing a Gothic novel, which ultimately is to thrill his reader.

Male characters

- **Dr Henry Jekyll** – the main protagonist, whose experiments result in separating his alter ego from his own self and hence the creation of **Mr Edward Hyde**.
- **Mr Gabriel John Utterson** – a lawyer and trusted friend of Dr Jekyll and Dr Lanyon. It is mostly through his eyes that the reader sees the story unfold.
- **Dr Hastie Lanyon** – an old friend and colleague of Dr Jekyll's, although recently estranged due to a non-specified professional disagreement.
- **Mr Poole** – Dr Jekyll's trusted and loyal butler, who turns to Utterson for help when he thinks Dr Jekyll's life is in danger.
- **Mr Guest** – Mr Utterson's trusted clerk and handwriting expert. He identifies the handwriting of Mr Hyde as being the same as Dr Jekyll's except that it slopes in the opposite direction.
- **Mr Richard Enfield** – Mr Utterson's distant relative, with whom he takes his regular Sunday walks. It is through his narrative that the reader encounters Hyde in the opening chapter.
- **'Sawbones'** – the doctor from Edinburgh who treats the small girl.

- **Sir Danvers Carew** – a benign old gentleman, Conservative Member of Parliament and client of Mr Utterson, who is beaten to death in cold blood by Mr Hyde.
- **Inspector Newcomen** – the police officer who accompanies Mr Utterson to Mr Hyde's lodgings and discovers the broken stick (the murder weapon) and the remnants of a burnt chequebook.
- **Bradshaw** – Dr Jekyll's footman.
- **Dr Denman** – the previous owner of Dr Jekyll's house and surgery/laboratory.

Female characters

- **The small girl** who is trampled by Hyde.
- **The maid** who witnesses the murder of Sir Danvers Carew. The stereotypical vulnerable female of the Gothic novel, a romantic dreamer who faints when she sees (and hears) the extreme violence of Hyde's unprovoked attack on Carew.
- **Mary, Dr Jekyll's maid,** and **the cook**, who whimpers hysterically and cries out when Poole returns to Jekyll's house with Utterson.
- **Edward Hyde's housekeeper**, 'An ivory-faced and silver-haired old woman. She had an evil face, smoothed by hypocrisy, but her manners were excellent.' She takes a strange delight, 'a look of odious joy', in learning Hyde is in trouble with the police.

The diagram below shows the connections between the characters.

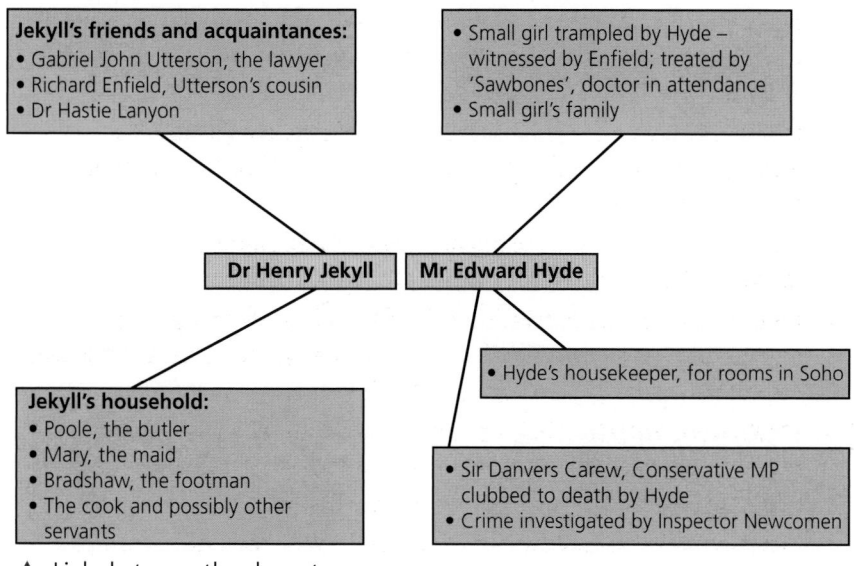

Jekyll's friends and acquaintances:
- Gabriel John Utterson, the lawyer
- Richard Enfield, Utterson's cousin
- Dr Hastie Lanyon

- Small girl trampled by Hyde – witnessed by Enfield; treated by 'Sawbones', doctor in attendance
- Small girl's family

Dr Henry Jekyll   **Mr Edward Hyde**

- Hyde's housekeeper, for rooms in Soho

Jekyll's household:
- Poole, the butler
- Mary, the maid
- Bradshaw, the footman
- The cook and possibly other servants

- Sir Danvers Carew, Conservative MP clubbed to death by Hyde
- Crime investigated by Inspector Newcomen

▲ Links between the characters

Main characters

Dr Henry Jekyll

Dr Jekyll is the most complex character. Stevenson introduces him positively. Dr Jekyll is 'a name well known and often printed' – according to Enfield – 'the very pink of proprieties'. Jekyll is a famous medical doctor and chemist, well known for his academic and philanthropic works.

Key quotation

'A large well-made, smooth-faced man of fifty, with something of a slyish cast perhaps.'

As soon as the reader is introduced to Jekyll in Chapter 3, there is a sense that he is not quite as he seems. The 'slyish cast' prepares the reader for the many aspects of Jekyll's character.

▲ Spencer Tracy as Jekyll, in the 1941 film

Jekyll seems a very genial socialite, regularly giving 'pleasant dinners' to his small group of respectable, discerning friends; yet Lanyon describes him, or at least his work methods, as 'fanciful'. In turn, Jekyll calls Lanyon 'an ignorant, blatant pedant', while at the same time agreeing with Utterson that Lanyon is an 'excellent fellow'. The reader could be forgiven for thinking there is a forced mood of gaiety in his conversation with Utterson, for as soon as Utterson mentions Hyde, Jekyll pales and his eyes blacken.

While Jekyll 'cherished for Utterson a sincere and warm affection', he is often less than honest with him (see Chapter 5 'The Incident of the Letter'). Nevertheless, he trusts Utterson with the safekeeping of his will and expects him to execute it should the need arise.

Stevenson devotes the whole of the last chapter to a detailed description of Jekyll and his actions. By 'allowing' Jekyll to speak for himself, the reader learns that Jekyll was born into a privileged sector of society; he is handsome, rich, popular and clever.

Jekyll found success easy to achieve and he is recognised as an expert in his field, yet there is a restlessness about him. He is aware that there is part of his nature that he is not fully able to express without restraint and he longs for freedom to indulge forbidden pleasures without feelings of guilt or fear of being found out. For this reason it is necessary to take into account Jekyll's alter ego, Edward Hyde.

Key quotation

'I saw that of the two natures that contended in the field of my consciousness, even if I could rightly be said to be either, it was only because I was radically both.'

Under the guise of serious scientific research (but really by accident) Jekyll manages to create a separate persona, which houses the evil side to his character and which, he maintains, acts independently from himself. Therefore Jekyll believes he bears no responsibility for Hyde's actions. It is only after Hyde kills Carew and Utterson appears to be close to the truth that Jekyll resolves never again to change into Hyde. He represses his bestial desires and as a result they intensify to the point that metamorphosis occurs spontaneously and Hyde becomes beyond Jekyll's control.

Build critical skills

Re-read what Stevenson makes Jekyll say about his own character at the beginning of Chapter 10. How far do you agree with his self-assessment? What effect does it have on you, the reader?

Key quotation

'I was in no sense a hypocrite...'

Key quotation

'...tales came out of the man's cruelty, at once so callous and violent, of his vile life, of his strange associates, of the hatred that seemed to have surrounded his career'

Build critical skills

What characteristics do you think Hyde shares with rats, snakes and apes? Select a quotation from the text to support your answer.

Edward Hyde

Stevenson uses Hyde to represent the beast in man; he is the fiend. He is a creature of the night, operating under the cover of darkness, delighting in inflicting pain. The reader is treated to only two episodes of his wicked behaviour: the trampling of the small girl and the savage murder of Danvers Carew. The rest are shrouded in secrecy. This secrecy helps to add to the atmosphere of terror. Clearly his crimes are unspeakable in Victorian society.

Hyde looks and sounds different from the other characters. The characters who have seen him fail to describe him adequately, but there is one thing upon which they are all agreed: that they were left with the impression that he was deformed in some way that they could not specify.

When analysing character and characterisation, it is usual to look at what characters do and say, and also what the writer has characters say about each other. Stevenson often attributes the characteristics of animals – rats, snakes and apes – to Hyde.

Enfield also compares him to Satan; Utterson says he has 'Satan's signature upon his face'. Compared with Jekyll, he is small, muscular, wiry and hairy, suggesting a less evolved, more primitive version of man. As the novel progresses, his power grows.

Build critical skills

The reader is never given a description of Hyde's face. Even Poole refers to him as 'wearing a mask'. Is this literal or metaphorical? What do you think Stevenson's intentions were in omitting this description?

Hyde's speech is curt and fragmented. He asks many short questions. He has no social graces. He is uncouth; he directly accuses Utterson of lying when they first meet. His speech patterns are very different from the other characters, who speak in a very elaborate style. Interestingly, when he is tantalising Lanyon into staying to watch him revert to the form of Henry Jekyll, he too adopts this elaborate style:

'And now, you who have so long been bound to the most narrow and material view, you who have denied the virtue of transcendental medicine, you who have denied your superiors – behold!'

The reader could be forgiven for believing this was Jekyll speaking, both in the content of what is said and how it is delivered. Some critics believe this was a mistake on Stevenson's part.

Mr Utterson

Stevenson himself describes the character of Utterson in some detail in the opening of Chapter 1 'The Story of the Door'. It is mostly through Utterson's eyes that the reader sees the events of the novel unfold in the first eight chapters. It would appear that it falls to Utterson to 'solve' the *Strange Case of Dr Jekyll and Mr Hyde*, as it was originally called.

Above all, Utterson is clearly shown to be loyal to his friends and clients and he does not judge them. Stevenson presents Utterson as a man who lives a moderate life and, although obviously very wealthy, he does not indulge in the luxuries of fine wine when alone, but drinks coarse gin instead. He is modest and 'austere' and does not indulge his feelings in any way, but endeavours to remain detached by attempting to rationalise human behaviour. There seems nothing remarkable about Utterson, yet he is a popular dinner guest among his circle of friends. He is mature and can control the baser part of his nature. Unlike Jekyll, he seems to do this by practising self-denial, as we are told he enjoys fine wines and visits to the theatre, but denies himself both most of the time.

In the novel, Utterson represents the conventional idea of a respectable Victorian gentleman, a person of refinement who is trustworthy, discreet and will go to great lengths to protect the reputations of his friends. He is presented as a very steady character who attempts to explain the significance of the events in the novel through common sense and reason, although Stevenson uses literary devices such as dreams in order to create suspense and a sense of the supernatural. Utterson, though, clings desperately to reason long after the reader has accepted the supernatural nature of events.

Strangely for a lawyer, Utterson does not indulge much in conversation even on his regular Sunday afternoon walks with Mr Richard Enfield, and he certainly does not indulge in idle gossip. Stevenson is perhaps suggesting that as a lawyer he understands the importance of preserving reputations at all costs, but he could also be suggesting that Utterson is a serious man of great integrity – a man whom the reader can also trust (see 'Themes', page 46). People noticed Utterson and Enfield hardly speaking to each other and both seemed to be relieved when they encountered friendly faces and stopped to chat. Yet Utterson was 'lovable', he was more likely 'to help rather than reprove' and this made him popular, even with hardened criminals. He was approachable and all the other characters confide their feelings and turn to him for help as the bizarre events unfold.

Utterson takes great pains to protect Jekyll from Hyde, as he assumes that Jekyll is being blackmailed regarding some unspecified youthful wrong-doing. As with his clients, he doesn't judge: 'I incline to Cain's heresy ... I let my brother go to the devil in his own way.' This shows he has a

Key quotation

'Mr Utterson the lawyer was a man of a rugged countenance, that was never lighted by a smile: cold scanty and embarrassed in discourse: backward in sentiment: lean, long, dusty, dreary and yet somehow lovable...'

Key quotation

Utterson felt 'humbled ... by the many ill things he had done', yet Stevenson describes his past as 'fairly blameless'.

self-deprecating sense of humour as the Bible clearly states that Cain murdered his brother, and although Utterson is aware that he may not be able to change what people do or what happens to them, he believes in redemption. God alone can judge and Christianity teaches that, provided a wrong-doer seeks forgiveness, he will be saved. Stevenson makes it clear that Utterson is the kind of person who will do his best to protect the innocent and be a source of comfort to his fellow men. He strives to avoid scandal and to protect the reputations of those he perceives to be worthy. The lengths to which he goes to avoid the breaking down of the door of Jekyll's laboratory in Chapter 8 symbolise his Victorian values. The upkeep of appearances is important to him above all else.

After Chapter 8, the narrative structure changes, as the truth regarding the strange case of Dr Jekyll and Mr Hyde is revealed in the last two chapters through 'Dr Lanyon's Narrative' and 'Henry Jekyll's Full Statement of the Case': documents left for Utterson to read after the deaths of his friends.

Richard Enfield

Utterson's young cousin makes only two appearances in the novel and yet he is an important character as it is through him that Stevenson gives the reader the first glimpse of Mr Hyde. He is introduced as 'the well-known man about town'. Like Utterson he is eminently respectable and a rationalist, and the two frequently enjoy each other's silent company on their Sunday strolls. It is on one of these walks that Enfield recounts the horror he felt when he witnessed Hyde collide with a young girl and proceed to trample over her body. He is so shaken by the event that he recalls the story but, as he is not given to idle gossiping, he leaves out the names of the people involved until Utterson requests the identity of the villain. He is horrified that Utterson is familiar with the owner of the house and vows never to mention the event again.

Build critical skills

Why do you think Enfield has difficulty in describing Hyde even though he spent several hours in his company? Compare his reaction with that of others who have met Hyde, particularly after Utterson takes Inspector Newcomen to Hyde's house in Soho after the Carew murder. Why does Stevenson leave these blanks in Hyde's description?

The reader next encounters Enfield in Chapter 7, the very short chapter where Utterson and Enfield, while out on their usual Sunday walk, encounter Jekyll at his window. They witness with horror Jekyll beginning spontaneously to metamorphose into Hyde. Although the expression of terror on Jekyll's face 'froze the very blood', neither Utterson nor Enfield acknowledges what is happening and the normally outgoing young man, with horror in his eyes, walks on in silence. This time there is no rational explanation, though Utterson is not yet ready to concede this, and Stevenson may be suggesting the strength of their reaction as Enfield, perhaps, is too afraid to speak.

Dr Hastie Lanyon

The role of Dr Lanyon is very important as it is through his intervention that Stevenson reveals the awful transformation of Jekyll into Hyde. He appears only twice in the course of the action: in Chapter 2 'The Search for Mr Hyde' and in Chapter 6 'The Remarkable Incident of Dr Lanyon'. Chapter 9 'Dr Lanyon's Narrative' is devoted entirely to the reproduction of his letter to Utterson, which was to be opened after his death and the death or disappearance of Jekyll.

Lanyon and Jekyll had been friends for many years but there had been a severe disagreement over scientific matters and, although they maintained their friendship on a superficial level, they were at odds. Lanyon describes Jekyll as being 'too fanciful for me … wrong in mind' and he describes Jekyll's work as 'unscientific balderdash'. For his part, Jekyll describes Lanyon as 'an ignorant, blatant pedant'.

From his flamboyant reception of Utterson, the reader is given the impression that Lanyon is a theatrical character who is very conscious of the impression he is creating. This, and the fact that he has never heard of Edward Hyde, is all we learn about Lanyon in Chapter 2.

In Chapter 6 we learn that Jekyll and Lanyon are not totally estranged, as Lanyon had attended the dinner party on 8th January at Jekyll's house. It was after this that Utterson called on Lanyon once more to voice concern over Jekyll. Lanyon's physical deterioration was astounding: 'The rosy man had grown pale; his flesh had fallen away; he was visibly balder and older.' He describes himself as doomed and visibly panics when Jekyll's name is mentioned. His life has been 'shaken to its roots'. He states theatrically that he has had a shock from which he will never recover. Three weeks later he is dead!

Stevenson uses the contrast between Lanyon's appearance in Chapter 2, where he describes him as 'hearty, healthy' with 'a boisterous and decided manner', and in Chapter 6 to indicate the impact of his 'shock'. He doesn't explain this shock, thus increasing the terror and tension for the reader.

All is revealed in Chapter 9. The duality of Lanyon's nature is shown here. Despite their disagreement, Jekyll turns to Lanyon in time of need and Lanyon agrees to help him. It is when Lanyon's pride, vanity and curiosity get the better of him and he chooses to witness Hyde's transformation that his destruction is confirmed. Lanyon is forced to face his own

Build critical skills

Make notes on what you learn in Chapter 7 about the theme of silence in relation to Stevenson's characters.

Key quotation

In Chapter 2 Lanyon is described as: 'a hearty, healthy, dapper, red-faced gentleman with the shock of hair prematurely white and a boisterous and decided manner.'

Build critical skills

What effect would the deterioration of Dr Lanyon have had on the Victorian reader? How does it add to the sense of terror in the novel?

hypocrisy and when he recognises the evil in Hyde he feels he has no choice but to give up on life, as he recognises the fiend within himself and literally loses the will to live. Clearly he has succumbed to the evil plan of Jekyll and Hyde as Jekyll extracts his revenge for the professional disrespect Lanyon showed him in the past.

The character traits that Lanyon shares with Utterson are pragmatism and rationality. He refuses to accept that the world is not governed by reason and dismisses the supernatural as fanciful. When faced with the awful truth, he no longer embraces life. He is a loyal friend, he agrees to help Jekyll and he does not gossip. He, like the other professional men in the novel, understands the importance of maintaining one's reputation and thus contributes to the conspiracy of silence.

Poole

Poole is Jekyll's loyal manservant, who has been with Jekyll for twenty years. Although a relative minor character, Poole is instrumental in moving along the action in the novel. Stevenson makes several references to him in the novel, mainly as a vehicle to say that Jekyll is not at home. It is Poole who unknowingly alerts Utterson to the fact that Jekyll lied about the delivery of the note allegedly from Hyde, and it is he who seeks Utterson's help when he believes his master has been murdered.

Poole's main function is to add to the atmosphere of horror and terror in the novel. Like Lanyon before him, his appearance has been greatly changed by terrible shock by the time he plucks up courage to seek Utterson's help. This adds to the atmosphere of secrecy and the fact that he is anxious to preserve Jekyll's reputation. He also provides detail relating to the search for the drug and the changes that have taken place within Jekyll's home since Hyde has been allowed free access.

The minor characters

Stevenson does not develop these characters. There is little or no characterisation. They are included to fulfil a purpose or a role and in most cases they are servants. Even Danvers Carew can be considered as a public servant and his only role is as a victim. The same point can be made about the small girl. Other roles include: Jekyll's maid, his housekeeper, his cook and Bradshaw, his footman; Hyde's housekeeper; 'Sawbones' the doctor; and the fainting maid who witnesses the Carew murder. Many of these fit Gothic stereotypes; others are just functional, such as Guest (Utterson's clerk), who happens to be an expert on handwriting, and Inspector Newcomen, who investigates the murder.

GRADE *FOCUS*

Grade 5

To achieve a Grade 5, students will develop a clear understanding of how Stevenson uses language, form and structure to create characters, supported by appropriate references to the text.

Grade 8

To achieve a Grade 8, students will examine and evaluate the way Stevenson uses language, form and structure to create characters, supported by carefully chosen and well integrated references to the text.

REVIEW YOUR LEARNING

(Answers are given on p. 101.)

1   All of the characters who have encountered Hyde agreed on one thing about him. What is it?

2   Who said this: 'There is a rather singular resemblance; the two hands are in many points identical, only differently sloped.'?

3   Who is 'embarrassed by discourse' and why might this be a big handicap in his profession?

4   In what ways might Jekyll and Lanyon be considered similar?

5   Edward Hyde is considered to be 'the beast in man'. What beasts is he likened to?

6   Jekyll maintains that he is not a hypocrite. Give one example showing why a reader might not agree.

7   There is an important difference between most of the male characters in the novel and all of the women portrayed. What is it?

8   Who was 'a well-known man about town' and what was his main function in the novel?

9   How does the maid at the window exemplify a stereotype of a Gothic novel?

10   Who was Dr Denman?

Target your thinking

- What is a theme? (**AO1**, **AO3**)
- What are the main themes in *Dr Jekyll and Mr Hyde*? (**AO1**, **AO3**)
- Why are themes so important in *Dr Jekyll and Mr Hyde*? (**AO1**, **AO3**)
- What is a motif? (**AO1**, **AO3**)
- What are the motifs that occur in *Dr Jekyll and Mr Hyde*? (**AO1**, **AO3**)

What is a theme?

In literature, a theme is an idea that a writer explores through the plot, structure, characters and descriptions in a novel. There are many themes or dimensions to *Dr Jekyll and Mr Hyde*. These include a religious dimension, although religion is not mentioned, and a sexual dimension, although sex is not mentioned either. A theme is usually something that the writer wants the reader to think about. In some instances, writers may hope that, as a result of thinking about a particular theme, the reader may reconsider their attitudes and this might influence their behaviour. Stevenson's genius enables the reader to bring his or her own ideas to the reading of the novel and to make parallels between the ideas explored in Victorian England and present-day society: human nature and scientific and technological advancement.

One of the best ways to understand *Dr Jekyll and Mr Hyde* is to concentrate on its themes. There are several different ways of categorising these, and in any interpretation of literary themes there is bound to be some overlap. The list below suggests how the main themes of *Dr Jekyll and Mr Hyde* might be grouped. Don't let this put you off having thoughts of your own, however, and be confident enough to express them if you feel that there is textual evidence to support your ideas. The themes discussed here are:

- the duality of human nature
- secrecy
- hypocrisy
- the beast in man
- reputation and silence
- rationalism and the supernatural
- violence and repression.

The duality of human nature

What it means to be human has been a central theme of literature throughout the ages and, with the advancement of time and the development of science and technology, the exploration of the evolution of mankind becomes more fascinating. In Judaeo-Christian cultures, the Bible is considered one of the first literary compilations to attempt to explain the existence of man and the contradictions in his character and behaviour. It begins with the story of creation and man's fall from grace, having been tempted to eat from the tree of knowledge in the Garden of Eden. For many this is seen as symbolic of lost innocence and as an explanation of the existence of good and evil within every single human being. Original Sin is an idea that Stevenson would have been very familiar with, coming from a Presbyterian background.

Good and evil are the ultimate opposites, but Stevenson's characters exemplify other, seemingly contradictory, traits. For example, in Chapter 1, Utterson the successful lawyer is 'embarrassed by discourse'. He appears to be a very dull character, yet he was 'lovable' and a very popular dinner guest. It is not only in terms of his characters that Stevenson explores this idea of duality, but also in his settings. Jekyll's residence has two doors: the back door – shabby and sinister, 'blistered and distained' – and the front door, befitting the opulent residence of a man of social standing. A similar contrast exists between the criminal activity that takes place in the half-deserted backstreets of London at night in the lamp-light and the vibrant activity of shopkeepers in the crowded streets during daytime. Many people believe that Stevenson incorporated into his novel the contrasts between the dark narrow dead-end streets of the Old Town part of Edinburgh and the elegant Victorian Gardens of the New Town where he grew up.

The struggle between good and evil is a popular theme in literature and it has been expressed in many ways. In *Dr Jekyll and Mr Hyde* it is explored through the character of Henry Jekyll.

In Chapter 10 'Henry Jekyll's Full Statement of the Case', Stevenson has Jekyll make sense of all the events of the novel that lead up to his (Jekyll's) suicide. This gives the reader a chance to consider whether or not they accept Jekyll's perspective or to form their own ideas about the reasons for his behaviour.

Jekyll explains that having been born into a privileged part of society, much was expected of him and he knew he had obligations to his respectable family, who had provided his large fortune and his education. (Note the parallels with Stevenson's own upbringing, but remember: do not draw any direct conclusions from this in your responses.) Jekyll recognises how fortunate he was to be hard-working and talented. He basked in the admiration of others, had good friends and every possibility of an 'honourable and distinguished future'. Yet he had what he termed 'a certain impatient gaiety of disposition', which Stevenson uses as a **euphemism** for the weaknesses in his character. Jekyll concludes that scientific investigation into this topic is only in its infancy and, while he is convinced 'that man is not truly one, but truly two', believes other scientists will come after him to prove that 'man will be ultimately known for a mere polity of multifarious, incongruous and independent denizens.' In other words man possesses not just two personalities, but several.

Euphemism: a pleasant way of describing something very unpleasant.

This 'other' side of Jekyll's character needs an outlet for expression and, while performing scientific experiments, he chances upon a formula that enables him to separate out aspects of his character – but it is not a neat division. Although Hyde is the embodiment of all the evil in Jekyll's character, Jekyll remains the same as before. In other words, at the beginning Jekyll remained in control and he could decide when and where to switch personalities in order to indulge in his unsavoury pleasures. If the situation had remained under his control he would have had the best of both worlds, but of course he couldn't keep control and his greed, his vanity and his urges gradually come to control him – to the extent that, in order to destroy the ever-growing power of his evil persona, he has to destroy himself.

▲ Fredric March as Jekyll/Hyde in Mamoulian's 1931 film

Jekyll says the duality of human nature is 'the hard law of life that lies at the root of religion, and is one of the most plentiful springs of distress.' Does Stevenson choose to explore this idea because he was grappling with the religious faith he was born into? Is Stevenson looking for justification of the existence of goodness and evil within the context of his new-found atheism? These are just some of the ideas you might consider, but remember not to draw any hard and fast conclusions. Marks can be gained by an awareness of more than one possibility or interpretation.

Build critical skills

Can you think of any circumstances where the killing of a human being might be acceptable? Does Stevenson present it as such at the end of the novel?

At the end of Chapter 8 'The Last Night', Poole and Utterson appear to precipitate the death of Jekyll, but when they finally break down the door to the laboratory it is the body of Hyde that they find twitching in the last moment of life. They then go searching for the body of Jekyll. Yet we know from Jekyll's own account that he has killed himself, not Hyde. This might raise some philosophical questions about the nature of suicide, which was, to many Christian sects at the time, the ultimate act of evil. To them it was considered to be throwing God's most precious gift back in His face – the unforgivable sin – by giving in to despair. You might also consider whether Stevenson is suggesting that killing is sometimes justifiable in order to rid the world of a great evil. This idea may be relevant to contemporary society regarding what to do about malign dictators.

Another aspect of this theme is that the creation of Hyde was purely random, for had Jekyll approached the experiment in a 'more noble spirit' he could have created 'an angel and not a fiend'. The theme of the duality of human nature is at the very core of the novel and gives readers much to think about that is of relevance to their own lives.

Key quotation

'*...man is not truly one, but truly two.*'

Secrecy

'Hyde' is itself a homophone of 'hide', suggesting something is secret or hidden from view, and this pun or play on words is a deliberate technique used by the writer. Critics have suggested that Stevenson would have pronounced Jekyll in the Scottish way, 'Jeekyll', which is suggestive of 'Seek ill' or even 'Seek all'. Apart from the obvious link to the childhood game this suggests a deeper connection between Utterson and Jekyll, as Utterson actually articulates that 'If he be Mr Hyde,... I shall be Mr Seek' as he embarks on his quest to unravel the secrecy behind 'the startling clauses of the will'. He is referring to Jekyll's instruction that upon his death (or prolonged disappearance), Hyde should be his sole heir.

It is also worth considering that Jekyll's original motive for his experiments was to 'seek out' and explore the limits of the 'evil side of my [his] nature.'

Ultimately, the effects of secrecy are presented as negative. The secrecy begins when Utterson and Enfield are out on their regular Sunday afternoon walk. When Enfield points to the door (see Motifs, page 49), the reader is not made aware of the nature of the building behind it or told whose door it is; neither is Enfield aware of its significance, though ironically Utterson knows its secrets.

Stevenson gives a very detailed description of the door and the building in the novel and it is believed to be a description of the actual residence and workplace of a real-life surgeon, John Hunter (1728–93), who accepted the bodies of executed prisoners and unidentified paupers for the (illegal) purpose of providing trainee doctors with practice at dissection (see the article 'Discovering Literature: Romantics and Victorians' on the British Library website, **www.bl.uk/romantics-and-victorians**). The men who delivered these bodies were grave-robbers. Medicine was considered a dubious profession at the time (hence the name 'Sawbones' for the doctor in the anecdote where the little girl is trampled). The law of the land reflected Christian religious beliefs, and bodies were buried in consecrated ground in the firm belief that they would be resurrected in all their glory on Judgement Day. Stevenson considered Hunter's to be a fitting residence to adopt as Jekyll's home and laboratory.

Stevenson builds the theme of secrecy into the dialogue between his characters. Once Utterson has established the name of the person who trampled the child he knows the door is the back entrance to Jekyll's house, but he doesn't tell Enfield and this information is also withheld from the reader until the next chapter.

Build critical skills

Re-read Chapter 6 'The Remarkable Incident of Dr Lanyon'. Consider how Stevenson builds an atmosphere of secrecy and write down any questions you might have at this point, for example: Why does Jekyll agree with Lanyon that they should not meet again?

Key quotation

Enfield on the topic of not asking questions: 'You start a question and it's like starting a stone … and some bland old bird is knocked on the head in his own back garden, and the family have to change their name.'

Hypocrisy: a pretence at having a quality (e.g. virtue) or holding a certain view, when really you do not.

A veil of secrecy covers the whole novel. Despite Jekyll trusting Utterson with the contents of his will, he does not say why. Several times when Utterson visits Jekyll's house throughout the course of the novel, he is refused entry and no explanation is given. Lanyon and Jekyll's relationship has been damaged over a disagreement about a professional matter, which is not elaborated on. Jekyll begs a favour from Lanyon under mysterious circumstances without explanation. Poole arrives at Utterson's house in a state of alarm, repeating 'I can bear it no more'; the full horror of the circumstances is not disclosed. The nature of Jekyll's vices is never disclosed. In fact, the mystery and terror of the whole plot is dependent on Stevenson's ability to withhold information, to suggest but not make explicit and to create characters who are discreet enough to keep secrets.

Key quotation

Jekyll talking about the contents of his will and the secret relationship with Hyde: 'I do not care to hear more … This is a matter I thought we had agreed to drop.'

Hypocrisy

The theme of **hypocrisy** is closely linked to those of secrecy, reputation and silence. Appearance was very important to Victorians and, like the duality of human nature, there was a duality in society that was kept hidden.

Many writers of the time wrote about the plight of the poor, suffering children, exploited workers, the harsh justice system, degradation and death. Stevenson, however, bases this novel largely on the lives of upper-middle-class men, the pillars of society: doctors, lawyers and peers of the realm like Danvers Carew. The Metropolitan Police was a relatively new institution (founded in 1822) and it might come as a surprise that a reputable lawyer like Utterson delayed reporting the death of Hyde/Jekyll at the end of the novel or that Jekyll should lie about the letter he had forged but alleged had been delivered by hand.

Both Utterson and Enfield seemingly deplore blackmail and Utterson is determined to help protect Jekyll from what he believes is damning information being used against him by Hyde. Yet in the very first chapter Enfield is proud of the fact that he and 'Sawbones' were, in effect, blackmailing Hyde into paying the trampled girl's family £100 compensation.

Dr Lanyon, despite having profoundly disagreed with the nature of Jekyll's experiments, is still willing to help Jekyll by procuring chemicals for him and operating under a veil of secrecy. There is an element of hypocrisy when he elects to stay and witness the transformation from Hyde to Jekyll. It could be said that in doing this Lanyon begins to understand the dual nature of man within himself and cannot live with the knowledge of his own hypocrisy, and that when he comes face to face with pure evil (Hyde), it is this knowledge that kills him.

There are many instances of hypocrisy among the minor characters; one example is the old woman at Hyde's residence in Soho, so obviously pleased when she finds out her master is in trouble. Stevenson describes her as having 'an evil face, smoothed by hypocrisy'. Even the policeman, Inspector Newcomen, is wondering how he can manipulate the investigation of the murder of Carew to further his own career. It would seem that all the characters who come into contact with Hyde have one thing in common, and that is a recognition of the evil present in Hyde, despite being unable to give a credible description of him. This perhaps reflects their inner knowledge of their own duality and awareness of their own hypocrisy. To recognise evil, you have to have known it.

The theme of hypocrisy cannot be separated from the theme of the duality of human nature and this is best exemplified by Jekyll's own account in Chapter 10. While attempting to give a frank analysis of his own character and balance his virtues against his vices, he excuses himself of the responsibility for Hyde's actions. 'It was Hyde, after all, Hyde alone that was guilty.' Some might say he is indulging in self-pity by suggesting that he is experimenting with these drugs for the good of humanity so that man might recognise his own nature: 'I knew well that I risked death.'

Jekyll almost turns this admission into a virtue as he takes the **moral** high ground by blaming any guilt he might feel on 'the exacting nature of my aspirations, rather than any particular degradation in my faults.' He goes on to say that 'Though so profound a double-dealer, I was in no way a hypocrite...'

The beast in man

Once again this theme overlaps with the duality of human nature but concerns only Hyde. It is worth noting that Charles Darwin (1809–82), the author of *On the Origin of Species* (1859), was a great influential scientist of the time. He established the theory of evolution, which stated that all species of life, including humans, descended from a common ancestor and developed according to a branching pattern, as a result of natural selection or survival of the fittest. *Homo sapiens* is considered by some to be the pinnacle of evolution to date, but as a species we are still evolving. Although today evolutionary theory is widely accepted as fact, in Stevenson's time it was extremely radical. It was directly opposed to Creationist Theory – that man is descended from Adam and Eve – which the Christian churches supported at that time. The idea that humans were related to animals gave rise to concern and pitted science against religion. It was considered heresy by some.

Moral: operating according to a code of conduct that chooses to do good. Immoral means choosing evil over good, and amoral means operating according to natural instincts of survival, having no awareness of the concepts of good and evil or right and wrong.

Build critical skills

Examine Jekyll's speech in Chapter 10 and decide how far you agree with Jekyll's analysis of his own character. It is worth recalling at this point that Hyde is the undiluted evil side of Jekyll's *own* character.

Troglodyte: a prehistoric form of man.

Build critical skills

Perhaps Stevenson's intention was to explore the different facets of the human personality. What might he be saying about Hyde's personality when he compares his appearance and behaviour with that of animals?

Hyde clearly represents the beast in man. When he is first introduced his appearance is described as '**troglodytic**', an idea with clear links to Darwin's theories.

When Jekyll metamorphoses into Hyde he appears 'much smaller, slighter and younger' and yet his countenance gives off an impression of 'deformity and decay'. Jekyll refers to him as 'the animal within me'. Utterson describes Hyde as hissing and snarling and having a 'savage laugh'. Poole says he moved 'like a monkey' and 'cried out like a rat' when he saw him. This signifies that Hyde is of a much lower order of creature and has no conscience. Hyde is also compared to an ape in Stevenson's description of his brutal murder of Carew: '... with ape-like fury, he was trampling his victim underfoot'.

After the murder of Carew, Hyde disappears; the reader is told that much of his dreadful past has been revealed, although other crimes he has committed are not explained.

Reputation and silence

The main characters in the novel are all upper-class professional men between middle and old age, who appear to be quite wealthy. In Victorian times, even more than today, respectability was of utmost importance. Sayings like 'a gentleman's word is his bond' and 'noblesse oblige' (nobility has obligations) were popular at the time. Any sniff of a scandal could ruin a man's reputation and even professional rivals were expected to be discreet. Although Jekyll and Lanyon have had a major disagreement, neither makes public the details nor indeed even shares the reason with Utterson, a mutual friend and himself the soul of discretion.

Utterson and Enfield, though related and great friends, go to pains to avoid gossip, which amusingly makes their Sunday walks rather silent encounters. Enfield ponders on whether or not to release Hyde's name as the child molester and concludes that he can, as clearly Hyde is not a gentleman; he will not, however, reveal the name of the eminent person who signed the cheque! It could be said that there was a sense of loyalty among gentlemen that did not extend to outsiders.

Utterson resolves to help Jekyll as he assumes that he is being blackmailed; he urges Jekyll to rethink the contents of his will but does not make his suspicions known. Nor does he tell the police that he suspects Jekyll is sheltering Hyde after the murder of Carew. He does not even confront Jekyll with the evidence concerning the handwriting in the note and the lies pertaining to its delivery. Silence must be preserved to protect reputations.

Reputation is shown to be important in the novel through the behaviour of Stevenson's characters. Appearances have to be maintained, and much of the action takes place under cover of darkness. There is a sordid side to Victorian society but so long as order and gentlemanly good manners prevail on the surface, the semblance of respectability and the reputations of individuals are maintained. Even at the very end of the actual story, in Chapter 8 'The Last Night', Utterson returns home to study the documents before letting the police loose at the scene of the crime (suicide was considered a crime until 1961, and people who attempted it could incur a penalty of up to fourteen years in prison!). This is a last-ditch attempt to preserve Jekyll's reputation as well as a reluctance on the part of Utterson to face the truth.

Rationalism and the supernatural

Rationalism explains what is happening in the world in terms of observation and experimentation, cause and effect. Events and changes are explained in terms of nature and development. Scientists like Jekyll and Lanyon observe, form hypotheses and theories, test them, and draw conclusions. Thus they explain happenings in terms of reason.

The supernatural, by definition, exists above (super) nature; another word for supernatural is transcendental, as it transcends (goes above) nature and explains phenomena in mystic or spiritual terms.

In *Dr Jekyll and Mr Hyde* the ultimate rationalist is Utterson. He goes to great lengths to explain the events of the novel in rational terms. He is convinced that Jekyll's troubles stem from being blackmailed. He is a lawyer and his mind is trained to deal with ideas only in terms of reason and common sense. He does not possess the imagination to understand Jekyll's real predicament.

Stevenson describes Utterson as 'a lover of the sane and customary sides of life, for whom the fanciful was the immodest.' The only way Stevenson can begin to draw Utterson into the very fringes of the supernatural is through a dream sequence, which spurs on Utterson to seek out Mr Hyde in the broad light of day. Even when Utterson comes face to face with the evil Edward Hyde and realises that there is no explanation for his disquietude or for the fear and loathing he feels, he continues to search for a rational explanation. He says, 'There must be something else.'

Long after the reader realises there is no rational explanation for the events, Utterson clings to his firm belief in reason. When faced with the real evidence at the end of Chapter 7 'The Incident at the Window', he still refuses to accept what is happening and instead hides behind a plea for God's forgiveness.

In Chapter 8 Utterson cross-examines Poole as though he is in court, creating a reasoned defence for Jekyll's behaviour, but in reality looking for every excuse not to break down the door to Jekyll's cabinet. It is only when faced with Jekyll's disappearance and the impossibility of his escape from the room that he admits, 'This is beyond me, Poole.' Even at this late stage he clings to the possibility of a rational outcome and returns home to study the documents before calling the police.

> **Build critical skills**
>
> Why does Stevenson present Utterson as a rationalist? Think about why, in modern horror films, there is often one person who refuses to believe that whatever is happening has a supernatural cause.

Lanyon, Jekyll's fellow scientist, is forced to accept the supernatural explanation for Jekyll's scientific experiments far sooner, since he actually observes Hyde's metamorphosis into Jekyll. He cannot live with this truth and goes into physical decline and eventually gives up on life.

Violence and repression

The themes in *Dr Jekyll and Mr Hyde* are all interlinked. The duality of human nature, the beast in man, and hypocrisy do not relate just to characters, they may be applied to wider Victorian society and also have implications relating to our views on modern society. Initially Jekyll rejoices in his transformation into Hyde as it gives him the perfect cover and freedom to express his innermost desires. It becomes apparent, however, that the more freedom Hyde has to express himself, the more violent his actions become. It is only when faced with the inevitability of being caught after the murder of Danvers Carew that Jekyll decides not to metamorphose into Hyde any longer.

It is important to remember that Hyde's physique is much smaller than that of Jekyll because it has not had the same length of time to evolve. Once evil is unleashed, however, it grows stronger and Jekyll's living nightmare begins when he realises that he no longer has any control over when or where Hyde may emerge. Indeed in Henry Jekyll's last statement it is clear that he takes a gamble. At the end of his life he is in grave danger of turning into Hyde permanently as he cannot accept that Hyde is part of his own nature and that by repressing him the level of violence is soaring. The point Stevenson is making is that the denial of both the darker side of human nature and of society's hypocrisy exacerbates the problem and leads Jekyll into choosing to take his own life rather than allowing the evil within to take control. It is the suppression of this dark side that can lead to certain violence and maybe it is an explanation of why barbaric crimes occur in society at large even in the present day.

Motifs

A motif is an idea or object that recurs throughout a literary work. It is different from a theme, which is a central idea, but a motif may be used to enhance our understanding of other themes and ideas. The main motifs in *Dr Jekyll and Mr Hyde* are:

- the door
- the mirror
- the idea of a mask; physical appearance
- light and dark; weather.

The door

Doors are symbolic as well as physical. They symbolise entrances and exits, acceptance or rejection. They are entrances not only to another physical environment but can metaphorically be seen as accessing different worlds. They are also barriers. Jekyll's residence has two doors. The front door is elegant and it is the gateway into a comfortable, safe, respectable home; the rear door is neglected, 'blistered and distained'. This door appears to be used solely by Hyde and it leads to the old, disused dissecting rooms in part of Jekyll's laboratory. The rear door does not represent the public respectable face of medicine but instead conjures up thoughts of rotting cadavers, human dissection and grave-robbers. The other significant door is the door to Jekyll's cabinet, which eventually is broken down by Utterson and Poole. This represents the breaking down of secrecy and ultimately the triumph of good over evil, as it is this action that precipitates the destruction of Jekyll but more importantly the death of Hyde. The motif of the door is used to emphasise the secrecy; it is Hyde's method of entry into Jekyll's residence.

Windows are used in a similar way. There are no windows on that side of the house and, where there are windows in the laboratory, they are barred. Visitors are not welcome.

In Chapter 8 'The Last Night', Utterson returns to Jekyll's house with the terrified Poole, who is convinced his master has been murdered. There is much prevarication but the climax of the chapter is when, at Utterson's bidding, Poole takes an axe to the red (signifying danger) baize door to the laboratory. This is a hugely symbolic action. All secrecy is shattered. Fear is overcome. Evil is about to be exposed and good will triumph.

The mirror

Poole and Utterson are surprised to find a cheval glass in Jekyll's cabinet and are curious as to why such a piece of furniture should have a place in a laboratory. They conclude that the mirror must have seen some strange things and they also see an image of their true (frightened) selves reflected back at them. The use of the mirror is revealed in the final chapter, where Jekyll admits he brought it into the laboratory so he could observe his transformation. When he looked in the mirror it was with a kind of pleasurable detachment. He welcomed his other self and recognised his evil nature, but at no time did he feel responsible for the actions of Hyde.

The idea of a mask; physical appearance

In Chapter 8 'The Last Night', Poole recounts to Utterson that he stumbled upon the occupant of the cabinet, whom he had thought was his master. It appears the occupant had momentarily left his confines

Build critical skills

Consider the significance of both barred windows and the absence of windows.

Re-read Chapter 7 'The Incident at the Window'. Then make notes on the effectiveness of the language used in the following short passage:

'The middle one of the three windows was half way open; and sitting close beside it, taking the air with an infinite sadness of mien, like some disconsolate prisoner, Utterson saw Dr Jekyll.'

Build critical skills

Consider any connection there may be between mirrors, doors and windows. How might they be significant when interpreting the writer's ideas?

Build critical skills

Consider which of the characters might be wearing a metaphorical mask. What might they be hiding? How do fog, mist and darkness mask the behaviour of Hyde?

to go in search of the drug. The person looked nothing like Jekyll, which led Poole to ask the question that if it were Jekyll, why was he wearing a mask? Always the person to look for a rational explanation, Utterson suggests that the reason for wearing a mask could be because Jekyll was suffering from a disease that had caused physical deformity. This is a great leap in logic, although in a metaphorical sense Jekyll has been wearing a mask of respectability to hide his true nature.

Another motif that appears at several points in the novel is the difference in size between Henry Jekyll and Edward Hyde. Apart from posing practical problems for the comings and goings of both these characters, this is of deep significance. At the end when Hyde's body is found, he is wearing the clothes of the much larger Henry Jekyll. This could symbolise that good has conquered evil and that it was a very close call. Had Hyde not been fatally weakened, Jekyll had considered alternative endings whereby Hyde tears up the will, faces the hangman's noose for the murder of Carew or commits suicide when cornered.

Light and dark; weather

Build critical skills

How does darkness or light help to create atmosphere in another part of the novel?

Stevenson connects the dark closely with secrecy. The two major acts of extreme violence happen at night, though the first is illuminated by street lamps. These would be gas-lamps, which created flickering shadows and shed very limited, yellow light compared to what we are used to today. The murder of Carew takes place under the light of the full moon. Stevenson creates visions of Hyde slipping in and out of the shadows, swiftly appearing and disappearing, walking at a pace through the shadows or disappearing into fog that rolled off the Thames in the small hours, turning up at Lanyon's residence at midnight in search of drug potions. It is not only Hyde who appears to operate at night. Utterson is fond of nocturnal visiting, Enfield offers no explanation for being on the streets in the early hours, and why Carew should be seeking directions in London at 11 p.m. as surmised by the innocent maid can only be left to the reader's imagination.

Yet London at the end of the nineteenth century was notorious for violent crime. Two years after the publication of *Dr Jekyll and Mr Hyde*, a stage-play version of the novel was interrupted by a demonstration accusing Stevenson of inciting Jack the Ripper to commit the Whitechapel murders.

Key quotation

The pathetic fallacy foreshadows Jekyll's death (see 'Language, style and analysis', pages 56–57): 'It was a wild, cold, seasonable night of March with a pale moon lying on her back as though the wind had tilted her.'

GRADE *FOCUS*

Grade 5

To achieve a Grade 5, students should reveal a clear understanding of the key themes of the novel and how Stevenson uses language, form and structure to explore them, supported by appropriate references to the text.

Grade 8

To achieve a Grade 8, students will examine and evaluate the key themes of the novel, analysing the ways that Stevenson uses language, form and structure to explore them. Comments will be supported by carefully chosen and well integrated references to the text.

REVIEW YOUR LEARNING

(Answers are given on p. 101.)

1 What is a theme?

2 How is a theme different from a motif?

3 What are the main themes in *Dr Jekyll and Mr Hyde*?

4 What might Stevenson's purpose be in exploring the theme of the duality of human nature?

5 What is the simile that Stevenson uses to describe the way Hyde trampled Carew?

6 How does Stevenson present the theme of rationalism and the supernatural? Express this in one or two sentences.

7 How does Stevenson maintain an atmosphere of secrecy?

8 What are the main motifs in *Dr Jekyll and Mr Hyde*? Express these in one sentence.

9 Outline the differences between the front and rear entrances to Jekyll's premises.

10 What might darkness and light symbolise?

Target your thinking

- What does the term 'style' refer to? (**AO2**)
- What narrative approaches does Stevenson adopt? (**AO2**)
- How does Stevenson use settings? (**AO2**)
- How does Stevenson make descriptions effective by his use of language? (**AO2**)
- How does Stephenson use symbolism? (**AO2**)

Anyone who has read *Dr Jekyll and Mr Hyde* will know what happens in the story, but as a serious student and literary critic you are expected to be able to analyse Stevenson's language and style and show that you understand the choices he had to make as a writer. Structure is covered in Chapter 3 of this guide.

Deconstructing a novel: pulling it apart critically to see what makes it successful. This involves looking at the language, the structure and the form in order to analyse how it has been constructed or put together.

Genre: a word borrowed from French, meaning type. There are many types or categories of novels, such as Gothic horror, romance and detective.

> **GRADE BOOSTER**
>
> Remember: it is not enough just to identify the methods used by the writer using the correct terminology. You must also explore the effects of these on the reader, and that is usually done by explaining how Stevenson's use of language and form are effective.

When you are writing about style you have to **deconstruct the novel** to show you appreciate that it is a construct and that it has been built to exemplify the writer's ideas as well as to tell a story. Your task is to 'unpick' the novel to show how it has been constructed to achieve the author's desired effects and to make it enjoyable for the reader.

Sometimes writers adopt a certain style that has been tried and tested. They are writing in a certain **genre**; in this instance, Stevenson wrote a horror story with elements of the Gothic novel (see 'Context', page 14).

> **GRADE BOOSTER**
>
> When writing about language, remember to choose individual words or short phrases for analysis. Longer phrases or even sentences make it difficult to focus sharply on the point you are making about the writer's choice. Examiners often prefer candidates to 'write a lot about a little'. That way you are sure to analyse rather than describe using generalities.

The list below gives some of the main features covered by the word 'style'. Stevenson made choices about all of them:

- form/viewpoint
- setting: time, place
- dialogue, conversation, and silence too!
- order of events
- withholding information
- names
- structural devices, e.g. letters, dreams, testimonies
- imagery
- symbolism.

Form

The form of a novel refers to the choices that the writer makes in terms of how he tells the story, or in other words the viewpoint. Stevenson could have written the whole of the story in the first person, in which case Utterson would be giving a blow-by-blow account of events from his point of view. This may have been rather tedious as we know his character to be rather dour and unimaginative. Instead, for the first eight chapters, Stevenson chooses to write in the third person (admittedly much of the time from Utterson's viewpoint), as this method allows him to include dialogue and a dream sequence and to maintain a sense of objectivity in order to allow the reader to interpret events and form his or her own opinion. This method also allows the author to include his own comments or to intrude in the narrative, for example: 'Now that the evil influence had been withdrawn, a new life began for Dr Jekyll.' This quotation exemplifies the way Stevenson imparts information by entering into the narrative.

By choosing this form, Stevenson allows the reader to see the different perspectives through the dialogue and the description of the thoughts and actions of the different characters. For instance, the reader learns of Hyde's first atrocity through Richard Enfield's eyewitness account in Chapter 1 'The Door'. Utterson's reaction to the event is shown through the dialogue, in what the reader is led to believe is one of their rare conversations.

The same anonymous third person continues to recall events, revealed mostly through the actions and dialogue between Utterson and other characters, until the end of Chapter 8 'The Last Night'. This gives authenticity to the story, as Utterson is a lawyer and therefore seen as dependable. Stevenson presents him as a man who is precise and accurate and not a man of ideas; neither does he possess a vivid imagination. He is down to earth, dull and trustworthy, and above all securely grounded in reality, and as such the reader can believe in him and in his judgement.

By structuring the novel in this way, Stevenson can avoid revealing too much information since the reader's knowledge is clearly restricted to the explanations of what the characters themselves witness and are prepared to accept. He can include descriptions of buildings, streets and the weather. The fact that most events happen late at night and in the early hours of the morning (apart from the Sunday afternoon walks of Utterson and Enfield) enables Stevenson to manipulate the reader's reaction by creating an atmosphere of secrecy, darkness and supernatural activity in order to add to the fear and horror experienced by the reader as the suspense builds. All this leads to a greater horror at the truth when it is revealed. The reader's worst fears are confirmed and finally Utterson can no longer hide behind increasingly implausible rational explanations of events.

Stevenson chooses to deliver Chapter 9 in the form of a letter from Lanyon to Utterson and Chapter 10 in the voice of Jekyll, again addressed to Utterson in the form of a statement. Hearing a voice in the first person allows the reader more freedom to interpret. The reader is familiar with the events that Lanyon is recalling in his letter, but Lanyon is giving them meaning. One outcome of this is that the reader comes to a better understanding of Lanyon's sudden decline and ultimate death. The reader at this point of the novel is completely familiar with the characters of Lanyon and Jekyll and is not being told what to think by Stevenson. For example, in the next chapter when Jekyll states, 'I am in no way a hypocrite', the reader will not necessarily agree.

The novel ends abruptly after Jekyll's testimony, which effectively is a suicide note. The reader is left to draw his own conclusions concerning the significance of events leading up to Jekyll's suicide. There is no more commentary from Utterson, no more attempts to rationalise events or to save Jekyll's credit or reputation. There is no natural explanation; the reader is left to contemplate a supernatural one.

By choosing to write in this particular form, Stevenson adds to the terror and horror of the tale. There is a climax, the story ends. We as readers do not know what happens next. Does Utterson return to Jekyll's residence and call the police? Does he eventually accept the events that have taken place are supernatural, or is he so entrenched in seeing life through his lawyer lens that he continues to rationalise what has happened? Do he and Poole come to an agreed interpretation of events? By the end of the novel the reader has been abandoned by all the characters and by Stevenson himself, and is left only with these chilling words:

'I bring the life of that unhappy Henry Jekyll to an end.'

GRADE **BOOSTER**

Don't be afraid to be critical of the ending Stevenson chooses, but always ensure you can support your view with evidence and close analysis.

Creating atmosphere

Descriptive language

Although the place and time where the novel is set is Victorian London, some critics believe that Stevenson's ideas of what London was like at this time were based on his home city of Edinburgh. In the 1820s in Edinburgh, Burke and Hare were alleged to have murdered sixteen people and sold the corpses to Dr Robert Knox for dissection in his anatomy classes. Interestingly, 'Sawbones' has an Edinburgh accent and is described as being 'as emotional as a bagpipe'. Edinburgh was also a city of great contrasts: of affluence and unmitigated poverty, fine architecture and squalid slums. These are exemplified in the contrasting aspects of Jekyll's immediate neighbourhood, which Stevenson describes in great detail: the thriving shops and the part of the street where the back entrance of his property 'thrust forward its gable onto the street.' The verb chosen is quite nasty and gives the air of intrusion.

The streets around Jekyll's house seem warm and friendly: 'the shop fronts stood along that thoroughfare with an air of invitation, like rows of smiling saleswomen…'; 'it shone … like a fire in the forest.' The use of these two **similes** gives a very welcoming feel to the area, while the **alliteration** of 'smiling saleswomen' and of 'fire' and 'forest' complement each other in adding brightness, when much of the description in the rest of the novel is centred round the almost ever-present fog and lamp-lit nights. Here Stevenson emphasises the attractiveness of the street by using well-chosen adjectives, such as 'florid' to describe its charms, and its 'freshly-painted' shutters and 'well-polished' brasses. In contrast, Jekyll's back wall is 'discoloured' and 'bore in every feature the marks of prolonged and sordid negligence.' His door is 'blistered and distained'. This is **symbolic** as it represents the activities that take place in secrecy beyond the door.

Language

Stevenson uses imagery or figurative language throughout the novel to create a variety of effects for the reader. For example, the maid watches Hyde 'break out in a great flame of anger' immediately prior to the murder of Carew, which indicates the intensity of his fury while also suggesting his potential for causing pain and destruction. At the end of Chapter 9, Lanyon describes his reaction to seeing Hyde transform into Jekyll as '…my mind submerged in terror'. This suggests that having leapt back in alarm, and being hemmed in by a wall, he is suffering from such extreme fright that it feels as if he is drowning, not in water but in terror, and is losing control. The only escape for him now is death. These **metaphors** create pictures or images in the reader's mind that bring the story to life.

Simile: a comparative phrase where something is said to be *like* something else in a particular way, and which contains the words 'like' or 'as'.

Alliteration: using words close to each other that begin with the same sound and usually (but not always) the same consonant, e.g. 'like a **f**ire in the **f**orest'. Many students believe, falsely, that examples of alliteration just have to begin with the same letter.

Symbol: a word, image or character that carries a wider meaning than its literal meaning. For example, Hyde represents evil, and darkness and fog represent secrecy.

Metaphor: an example of figurative language where a writer says something is something else by way of comparison.

Build critical skills

Lanyon's 'life is shaken to its roots' when he witnesses Hyde transform into Jekyll. Analyse the effectiveness of this metaphor in the way shown by the two examples on page 55.

Pathetic fallacy: a term coined by John Ruskin, a great writer in the nineteenth century, to describe a setting, and particularly the weather, paralleling human qualities.

GRADE **BOOSTER**

You need to demonstrate some knowledge of technical terms when writing about language, but merely identifying language features will gain few marks. It is useful to use the correct terms when explaining the effect of language used, but all is not lost if you cannot remember the technical term as many marks can be gained by analysing the effects of a language feature by in-depth analysis of individual words or short phrases.

Pathetic fallacy

Pathetic fallacy, the literary tradition of the weather heralding events of the plot, is a well-established device.

The night Hyde tramples the small girl is described as 'black'. The night Utterson tracks down Hyde is 'a fine dry night: frost in the air, the streets as clean as a ballroom-floor; the lamps, unshaken by any wind.' On the night Danvers Carew is murdered, the early part of the night is cloudless and the lane is brilliantly lit by the full moon. This enables the maid to have a clear view of the terrible crime and its perpetrator, whom she recognises.

Through the description of Utterson's cab journey to Hyde's Soho residence with Inspector Newcomen, Stevenson creates a blanket of secrecy around the streets of the capital. 'The **f**irst **f**og of the season' rolls in off the river, wrapping the event in secrecy. The alliterative 'f' here adds to the sense of mystery. 'A great chocolate-coloured pall lowered over heaven'; the swirls of the fog are described in different shades of brown – 'a rich lurid brown', 'as brown as umber' – to match Utterson's thoughts, which are 'of the gloomiest dye' as he takes the policeman to Hyde's house. London fogs were like nothing experienced today. The air was literally brown and Stevenson draws the comparison with Utterson's dark thoughts. Another word for 'pall' is a shroud, which fits in with creating an image of death and a feeling of oppression as it is 'lowered over heaven' (a metaphorical expression meaning they could not see the sky). It suggests that the murder was an affront to God and therefore had to be screened. The fact that 'the wind was charging and routing' reflects the violence of Hyde and adds to the atmosphere of unease and disquiet, while simultaneously creating quite a wonderful eerie scene. 'Mr Utterson beheld a marvellous number of degrees and hues of twilight' as daylight tried to break through. This descriptive paragraph ends with an effective simile likening the place to 'a district of some city in a nightmare'. The description taken as a whole gives London a surreal quality.

▲ Scene from the 1941 film starring Spencer Tracy

In Chapter 8 'The Last Night', Poole returns with Utterson to Jekyll's home during a storm:

> 'It [the wind] seemed to have swept the streets unusually bare of passengers. … The square … was all full of wind and dust, and the thin trees in the garden were lashing themselves against the railings.'

The use of pathetic fallacy here shows the wind personified and the turmoil created by the storm reflecting the turmoil within the two men as they anticipate what they might find in Jekyll's cabinet. Both are consumed by terror and this is reflected in the strong and unpredictable winds that change direction.

The ideas of darkness and fog, lamplight and changing seasons, contrast of light and shadows, gloom and brilliant light, are all symbolic throughout the novel. Where darkness and fog appear it is generally to cover some shameful act or to shroud events in secrecy.

Dialogue

Stevenson creates **dialogue** to match the character of the people speaking. One of the most interesting relationships is that between Enfield and Utterson. Utterson speaks in a simple, calm way when he is interrogating Enfield regarding Hyde and his disappearance through the door, just as one might imagine a lawyer proceeding in cross-examination. When he is under pressure, however, Utterson becomes increasingly alarmed and this is reflected in his minimal use of

Dialogue: conversation between characters that adds to the reader's knowledge of what is happening.

words: 'Down with the door, Poole!' This is apparent when he eventually accepts that he is conversing with Hyde, not Jekyll, behind the locked door of the cabinet. At other times he appears to be master of the understatement: 'We have come too late' is his simple reaction on finding the corpse in the cabinet.

On the other hand Enfield, the 'well-known man about town', is much more flamboyant and verbose. His descriptions are long and detailed and once he embarks on his tale of the small girl who was trampled he is silenced only when he realises his own garrulousness. He is the complete opposite of Utterson. Most of the time, however, the pair seem to be content with companionable silences, which provide the occasional touch of humour to the text.

Hyde's speech is not like that of the other characters, which signifies he is not a gentleman in any way. When Utterson seeks him out, Hyde is abrupt and coarse. He fires a lot of questions at Utterson and accuses him of lying. He hisses, he cries, he snarls. These verbs fit in with the animal imagery ascribed to him. Throughout the text it is suggested that he moves like a monkey, cries out like a rat and hisses like a snake. Only when Hyde confronts Lanyon – just before he changes back to Jekyll – does he launch into an elaborate, stylish speech of triumph, which is very uncharacteristic.

Poole's speech, on the other hand, has much in common with that of Inspector Newcomen. They are not educated gentlemen and this shows as occasionally their speech is ungrammatical and their vocabulary limited compared to that of the professional gentlemen.

GRADE *FOCUS*

Grade 5

To achieve a Grade 5, candidates will show a clear appreciation of the methods Stevenson uses to create effects for the reader, supported by appropriate references to the text.

Grade 8

To achieve a Grade 8, candidates will explore and analyse the methods Stevenson uses to create effects for the reader, supported by carefully chosen and well integrated references to the text.

REVIEW YOUR LEARNING

(Answers are given on p. 102.)

1 What does the term 'form' refer to?

2 From what narrative perspective is the majority of the story of *Dr Jekyll and Mr Hyde* narrated?

3 What is alliteration?

4 Name two types of imagery Stevenson uses.

5 Explain the term 'pathetic fallacy'.

6 What is a symbol?

7 How does the language of working-class people differ from that of gentlemen in the novel?

8 Give an example from the text of a powerful verb and a powerful adjective, and explain how they are effective.

9 One speech of Hyde's stands out as being different from the rest. Which is it?

10 Why should you strive to 'write a lot about a little'?

Target your thinking

- What sorts of questions will you have to answer?
- What is the best way to plan your answer?
- How can you improve your grade?
- What do you have to do to achieve the highest grade?

Your response to a question on *Dr Jekyll and Mr Hyde* will be assessed in a 'closed book' English literature examination, which means that you are not allowed to take a copy of the examination text into the examination room. Different examination boards will test you in different ways and it is vital that you know on which paper the nineteenth-century novel will be, so that you can be well prepared on the day of the examination.

All four major examination boards offer *Dr Jekyll and Mr Hyde* for assessment. Check with your teacher which board you are being entered for and read the appropriate section below.

AQA

You will be required to answer one question on *Dr Jekyll and Mr Hyde* in Section B of Paper 1. The question will be based on a given extract and then you will be asked to write on the same topic in relation to the novel as a whole. There will be no choice of question on this novel. You will have approximately 50 minutes to complete your answer.

In total 30 marks will be available: 12 marks for Assessment Objective 1, 12 marks for AO2 and 6 marks for AO3. *Dr Jekyll and Mr Hyde* will **not** be assessed for AO4 with AQA.

You will be awarded a mark out of 30 and your answer will be marked holistically. These 30 marks are divided into six levels and the examiner will award you a level depending on your achievement. The top of Level 6 will equate to Grade 9, the highest award. Levels can never be tied exactly to grades, however, as they can change slightly from year to year.

Further useful information is available at **www.aqa.org.uk**, along with sample assessment papers and mark schemes.

Edexcel

You will be required to answer one question on *Dr Jekyll and Mr Hyde* in Section A of Paper 2. There will be no choice of question. The question will be in two parts. The first part will be focused on an extract from the novel of approximately 400 words, and the second part will be an essay question exploring the topic *elsewhere* in the text. A mark out of 20 will be awarded for each part.

In total 40 marks will be available: 20 marks for Assessment Objective 1 and 20 marks for AO2. *Dr Jekyll and Mr Hyde* will **not** be assessed for AO3 and AO4 with Edexcel.

These 40 marks are divided into five levels and the examiner will award you a level depending on your achievement. The top of Level 5 will equate to a Grade 9, the highest award. Levels can never be tied exactly to grades, however, as they can change slightly from year to year.

Further useful information is available at **http://qualifications.pearson.com**, along with sample assessment papers and mark schemes.

OCR

You will be required to answer one question on *Dr Jekyll and Mr Hyde* in Section B of Paper 1. There will be a choice of question. You can answer the extract-based question making links to elsewhere in the text, *or* you can choose the discursive essay question that requests you to explore at least two moments from the novel to support your ideas. Both answers will be marked holistically.

In total 40 marks will be available, which constitutes 25 per cent of the total for the English literature GCSE. Assessment Objectives 1–4 will be assessed and are weighted as follows:

- AO1 = 8.75 per cent
- AO2 = 8.75 per cent
- AO3 = 5 per cent
- AO4 = 2.5 per cent
- Total for the question = 25 per cent.

You will be awarded a mark out of 36 and your answer will be marked holistically for AOs 1, 2 and 3. These 36 marks are divided into six levels and the examiner will award you a level depending on your achievement. A further 4 marks are available for AO4. The top of Level 6 will equate to Grade 9, the highest award. Levels can never be tied exactly to grades, however, as they can change slightly from year to year.

Further useful information is available at **www.ocr.org.uk/qualifications/ gcse-english-literature-j352-from-2015**

WJEC/Eduqas

You will be required to answer one question on *Dr Jekyll and Mr Hyde* in Section B of Component 2. The question will be based on a given extract and then you will be asked to write on the same topic in relation to the novel as a whole. There will be no choice of question on this novel. You will have approximately 45 minutes to complete your answer.

In total 40 marks will be available. Assessment Objectives 1, 2 and 3 will be assessed. *Dr Jekyll and Mr Hyde* will **not** be assessed for AO4 with WJEC/Eduqas.

You will be awarded a mark out of 40 and your answer will be marked holistically. These 40 marks are divided into five bands and the examiner will award you a grade depending on your achievement. The top of Band 5 will equate to Grade 9, the highest award. Levels can never be tied exactly to grades, however, as they can change slightly from year to year.

Further useful information is available at **www.eduqas.co.uk**, along with sample assessment papers and mark schemes.

At a glance

Exam board	AQA	Edexcel	OCR	WJEC/Eduqas
Type of question	Extract-based initially then widens to include the novel as a whole.	Extract-based initially then widens to include other parts of the novel.	Extract-based initially then widens to include other parts of the novel. Alternative discursive question can be chosen.	Extract-based initially then widens to include the novel as a whole.
Closed book?	Yes	Yes	Yes	Yes
Choice of question?	No	No	Yes	No
Paper and section	Paper 1 Section B	Paper 2 Section A	Paper 1 Section B	Component 2 Section B
Time allowed for question	50 minutes	55 minutes	45 minutes	45 minutes
AOs assessed	AO1, AO2, AO3	AO1, AO2	AO1, AO2, AO3, AO4	AO1, AO2, AO3
Is AO4 (SPaG) assessed in this section?	No	No	Yes, 1.25% of the whole grade	No
% of whole grade	20%	25%	25%	20%

Marking

The marking of your responses varies according to the board your school or you have chosen. Each exam board has a slightly different mark scheme, consisting of a ladder of levels. The marks you achieve in each part of the examination will be converted to your final overall grade. Grades are numbered from 1–9, with 9 being the highest.

It is important that you familiarise yourself with the relevant mark scheme(s) for your examination. After all, how can you do well unless you know exactly what is required?

Assessment Objectives for individual assessments are explained in the next section of the guide (page 72).

Approaching the examination question

First impressions

First, read the whole question and make sure you understand *exactly* what the task requires you to do. It is very easy in the highly pressured atmosphere of the examination room to misread a question – and this can be disastrous. Under no circumstances should you try and twist the question to the one that you have spent hours revising or the one that you did brilliantly on in your mock exam!

Are you being asked to think about how a character or theme is being presented, or is it a description of a place? Make sure you know so that you will be able to sustain your focus later.

As a starting point, it is a good idea to underline or highlight keywords in the question, such as 'how' to remind you to write about methods, and any other words that you feel will help you to focus on answering the question you are being asked.

Look carefully at any bullet points you are given in the question. They are there to help and guide you, but don't restrict your answer entirely to them. Remember to consider the question and the text as a whole.

The four boards that offer *Dr Jekyll and Mr Hyde* as a text all use an extract-based question. The wordings and formats of the questions, however, are slightly different. (OCR additionally offers a discursive essay-type question. Seek advice from your teacher regarding which question to choose.)

For example, have a look at this extract, which could be used in a question set by any of the four boards:

It chanced on one of these rambles that their way led them down by a street in the busy quarter of London. The street was small and what is called quiet, but it drove a thriving trade on the weekdays. The inhabitants were all doing well, it seemed, and all emulously hoping to do better still, and laying out the surplus of their gains in coquetry; so that the shop fronts stood along that thoroughfare with an air of invitation, like rows of smiling saleswomen. Even on a Sunday, when it veiled its more florid charms and lay comparatively empty of passage, the street shone out in contrast to its dingy neighbourhood, like a fire in a forest; and with its freshly painted shutters, well-polished brasses, and general cleanliness and gaiety of note, instantly caught and pleased the eye of the passenger.

Two doors from one corner, on the left hand going east, the line was broken by the entry of the court; just at the that point, a certain sinister block of building thrust forward its gable on the street. It was two storeys high; showed no window, nothing but the door on the lower storey and a blind forehead of discoloured wall on the upper; and bore in every feature the marks of prolonged and sordid negligence. The door, which was equipped with neither bell nor knocker, was blistered and distained. Tramps slouched into the recess and struck matches on the panels; children kept shop upon the steps; the schoolboy had tried his knife on the mouldings; and for close on a generation no one had appeared to drive away these random visitors or to repair their ravages.

Mr Enfield and the lawyer were on the other side of the by street; but when they came abreast of the entry, the former lifted up his cane and pointed.

'Did you ever remark that door?' he asked; and when his companion had replied in the affirmative, 'It is very connected in my mind,' added he, 'with a very odd story.'

'Indeed!' said Mr Utterson, with a slight change of voice, 'and what was that?'

Below you can see examples of the question types from each examination board, with the keywords underlined.

AQA

Starting with this extract, <u>how</u> does Stevenson present the <u>setting</u> of Victorian London in the novel?

Write about:

- <u>how</u> Stevenson presents the <u>setting</u> of Victorian London <u>in the extract</u>
- <u>how</u> Stevenson presents the <u>setting</u> of Victorian London <u>in the novel as a whole</u>.

Eduqas

You should use the extract and your knowledge of the whole novel to answer this question.

Write about the <u>ways settings are described</u> throughout the novel.

In your response you should:

- refer to the extract and the <u>novel as a whole</u>
- show your understanding of the ways settings are used in the novel
- refer to the <u>contexts of the novel</u>.

Alternatively, have a look at this extract, which could also be used in a question set by any of the four boards.

As soon as he got home, Utterson sat down and wrote to Jekyll, complaining of his exclusion from the house, and asking the cause of this unhappy break with Lanyon; and the next day brought him a long answer, often very pathetically worded, and sometimes darkly mysterious in drift. The quarrel with Lanyon was incurable. 'I do not blame our old friend,' Jekyll wrote, 'but I share his view that we must never meet. I mean from henceforth to lead a life of extreme seclusion; you must not be surprised, nor must you doubt my friendship, if my door is often shut even to you. You must suffer me to go to my own dark way. I have brought on myself a punishment and a danger that I cannot name. If I am the chief of sinners, I am the chief of sufferers also. I could not think that this earth contained a place for sufferings and terrors so unmanning and you can do but one thing, Utterson, to lighten this destiny, and that is to respect my silence.' Utterson was amazed; the dark influence of Hyde had been withdrawn, the doctor had returned to his old tasks and amities; a week ago, the prospect had smiled with every promise of a cheerful and honoured age; and now in a moment, friendship and peace of mind and the whole tenor of his life were wrecked. So great and unprepared a change pointed to madness; but in view of Lanyon's manner and words, there must lie for it some deeper ground.

Edexcel

a   Explore how Stevenson presents the character of Jekyll in this extract.
Give examples from the extract to support your ideas.

b   In this extract, a detailed portrayal of Jekyll is created.
Explain why Jekyll is important **elsewhere** in the novel.
In your answer you must consider:

- the role of Jekyll in the novel
- how Stevenson presents Jekyll.

OCR

Explore how Stevenson presents mystery and suspense through the presentation of Jekyll in this extract and **elsewhere** in the novel.

OR:

The Strange Case of Dr Jekyll and Mr Hyde is an exploration of the nature of good and evil. How far do you agree with this view? Explore at least two moments in the novel to support your ideas.

Spot the differences!

- AQA and Eduqas both refer to the 'whole novel'.
- Edexcel and OCR use the phrase 'elsewhere in the novel'.
- Only Eduqas refers directly to 'contexts' in the question.
- Only Edexcel does not assess AO3 in this section.
- Only Edexcel divides its question into two separate sections, a) and b).
- Only OCR offers a choice of question.

Important

All four boards assess both AO1 and AO2 in this section of the paper. Always make sure you cover both of these AOs in your response, even if they do not seem to be clearly signposted in the question!

Except for one type of OCR question, whichever exam board you are taking you will be required to read a passage, so your next step is to read the passage very carefully, trying to get an overview or general impression of what is going on, and what or who is being described.

'Working' the text

Now *read* the passage again, underlining or highlighting any words or short phrases that you think might be related to the focus of the question and are of special interest. For example, they might be surprising, unusual or mysterious. You might have a strong emotional or analytical reaction to them or you might think that they are particularly clever or noteworthy.

These words/phrases may work together to produce a particular effect, or to get you to think about a particular theme, or to explore the methods the writer uses to present the setting in a particular way for their own purposes. You may pick out examples of literary techniques such as lists or use of imagery, or sound effects such as alliteration or onomatopoeia. You may spot an unusual word order, sentence construction or use of punctuation. The important thing to remember is that when you start writing you must try to *explain the effects* created by these words/ phrases or techniques, and not simply identify what they mean. Above all, ensure that you are answering the question that has been asked.

Planning your answer

It is advisable to write a brief plan before you start writing your response to avoid repeating yourself or getting in a muddle. A plan is not a first draft. You will not have time to do this. In fact, if your plan consists of any full sentences at all, you are probably eating into the time you have available for writing a really insightful and considered answer.

A plan is important, however, because it helps you to gather and organise your thoughts, but it should consist of only brief words and phrases.

You may find it helpful to use a diagram of some sort – perhaps a spider diagram or flow chart. This may help you keep your mind open to new ideas as you plan, so that you can slot them in. Arranging your thoughts is then a simple matter of numbering the branches in the best possible order. Or you could make a list instead. The important thing is to choose a method that works for *you*.

The other advantage of having a plan is that if you run out of time, the examiner can look at the plan and may be able to give you an extra mark or two based on what you were about to do next.

Writing your answer

Now you are ready to start writing your answer. The first thing to remember is that you are working against the clock and so it's really important to use your time wisely.

It is possible that you may not have time to deal with all of the points you wish to make in your response. If you simply identify several language features and make a brief comment on each, you will be working at a fairly low level. The idea is to select the ones that you find most interesting and develop them in a sustained and detailed manner. In order to move up the levels in the mark scheme, it is important to write a lot about a little, rather than a little about a lot.

You must also remember to address the whole question as you will be penalised if you fail to do so.

If you have any time left at the end of the examination, do not waste it! Check carefully that your meaning is clear and that you have done the very best you can. Look back at your plan and check that you have included all your best points. Is there anything else you can add? Keep thinking until you are told to put your pen down!

Referring to the author and title

You can refer to Stevenson either by name (make sure you spell it correctly) or as 'the writer' or 'the author'. You should never use his first name (Robert) – this sounds as if you know him personally. You can also save time by giving the novel title in full the first time you refer to it, and afterwards simply referring to it as 'the novel'.

GRADE BOOSTER

Do not lose sight of the author in your essay. Remember that the novel is a construct – the characters, their thoughts, their words, their actions have all been created by Stevenson – so most of your points need to be about what Stevenson might have been trying to achieve. In explaining how his message is conveyed to you (for instance through an event, something about a character, use of symbolism, personification, irony and so on), don't forget to keep mentioning the author's name as this will keep you on track to address AO2. For example:

- Stevenson makes it clear that…
- It is evident from … that Stevenson is inviting the audience to consider…
- Here, the audience may well feel that Stevenson is suggesting…

Writing in an appropriate style

Remember that you are expected to write in a suitable *register*. This means that you need to use an appropriate style. This means:

- do *not* use colloquial language or slang, e.g. 'Hyde is a nasty piece of work. A bit of a toe-rag really.' (The only exception is when quoting from the text, and you will be hard pressed to find slang in this novel!)
- do *not* become too personal, e.g. 'Robert didn't get on with his dad 'cos he was too religious.'
- *do* use phrases suitable for an academic essay, e.g. 'It could be argued that…', *not* 'I reckon that…'
- do *not* be too dogmatic. Don't say 'This means that…' It is much better to say, 'This might suggest that…'

GRADE *BOOSTER*

If you can't decide whether a phrase is a simile or a metaphor, it helps to just refer to it as an example of imagery and explain how the author wants the reader to respond to the word-picture he is painting.

You are also expected to be able to use a range of technical terms correctly. If occasionally you can't remember the correct name for a technique but can still describe it, you should go ahead and do so – as long as you explain the effects created you will gain marks.

The first person ('I')

It is perfectly appropriate to say 'I feel' or 'I think'. You are being asked for *your* opinion. Just remember that you are being asked for your opinion about *what* Stevenson may have been trying to convey in his novel (his themes and ideas) and *how* he does this (through the characters, events, language, form and structure of the novel).

Spelling, punctuation and grammar (AO4)

Although your spelling, punctuation and grammar are specifically targeted for assessment on the nineteenth-century novel *only* if you are sitting your exam with OCR, you cannot afford to forget that you will demonstrate your grasp of the novel through the way you write, so take great care with this and don't be careless. If the examiner cannot understand what you are trying to say, they will not be able to give you credit for your ideas.

How to raise your grade

GRADE *BOOSTER*

It is important to make the individual quotations you select brief and to try to *embed* them. This will save you time, enabling you to develop your points at greater depth and so raise your grade.

The most important advice is to answer the question that is in front of you, and you need to start doing this straight away. When writing essays in other subjects, you may have been taught to write a lengthy, elegant introduction explaining what you are about to do. You have only a short time in the literature examination, however, so it's best to address the task immediately, as soon as you have gathered your thoughts together and made a brief plan. Do not preamble by setting out what you are going to do... just do it!

Sometimes students panic because they don't know how to start. It is absolutely fine to begin your response with the words, 'In this extract Stevenson presents...', because whichever exam you are taking, you need to start with the author (unless of course you choose the discursive option with OCR).

Begin by picking out interesting words/phrases and unpicking or exploring them within the context or focus of the question. For example, if the question is about the way that evil is presented, you need to focus on picking out words and phrases to do with fear and tension and cruelty.

What methods has the writer used? Although there is a whole range of methods with which you need to be familiar, it might be something as simple as a powerful adjective. What do you think is the impact of that word? It might be that the word you are referring to has more than one meaning. If that's the case, the examiner will be impressed if you can discuss what the word means to you, but can also suggest other meanings. Is context relevant here? In other words, would readers in Stevenson's day have viewed evil differently? What might Stevenson have been trying to express about evil when he chose a particular word or phrase?

It is likely that you will find it easier to address AO2 (methods) when writing about the extract as you have the actual words to hand.

Is there an actual overall effect? For instance, you may have noticed Stevenson's frequent use of lists of phrases separated by semi-colons, which create intensely vivid impressions. In this case, as well as analysing individual words in the list (not necessarily all of them – just the most interesting ones) you could also describe the cumulative effect.

Be very careful about lapsing into narrative. If you are asked about how Stevenson presents Hyde, remember that the focus of the question is about the *methods* that Stevenson uses. Do not simply tell the examiner what Hyde does or what he is like; this is a very common mistake and will not help you hit the descriptors for the higher levels in the mark scheme.

Remember you also have to deal with the focus of the question in the novel as a whole, or in the case of Edexcel and OCR 'elsewhere in the novel.' You will be penalised if you do not do this so you **must** leave time. If you feel you have more to offer in terms of comments on the extract, leave a space so that you can return to it if necessary.

Key points to remember

- Do not just jump straight in! Spending time planning in those first moments may gain you extra marks later.
- Write a brief plan; practise making plans in spider diagram form before the exam. Number your ideas in the order you intend to present them.
- Remember to begin to answer the question right from the start; don't preamble.
- Refer closely to *details* in the passage in your answer, support your comments, and remember you must also refer to the novel as a whole (or refer to 'elsewhere' in the novel for Edexcel and OCR).
- Use your time wisely! Try to leave a few minutes to look back over your work and check your spelling, punctuation and grammar, so that your meaning is clear and so that you know that you have done the very best you can.
- Keep an eye on the clock!

GRADE *FOCUS*

Grade 5

- Candidates have a clear focus on the text and the task and are able to 'read between the lines'.
- Candidates develop a clear understanding of the ways in which writers use language, form and structure to create effects for the readers.
- Candidates use a range of detailed textual evidence to support comments.
- Candidates use understanding of the idea that both writers and readers may be influenced by where, when and why a text is produced.

Grade 8

- Candidates produce a consistently convincing, informed response to a range of meanings and ideas within the text.
- Candidates use ideas that are well linked and often build on one another.
- Candidates dig deep into the text, examining, exploring and evaluating the writer's use of language, form and structure.
- Candidates carefully select finely judged textual references that are well integrated in order to support and develop responses to texts.
- Candidates show perceptive understanding of how contexts shape texts and responses to texts.

Achieving a Grade 9

To reach the very highest level you need to have thought about the novel more deeply and produced a response that is conceptualised, critical and exploratory at a deeper level. You might, for instance, challenge accepted critical views in evaluating whether the writer has always been successful. If, for example, you think Stevenson set out to create fear and tension, how successful do you think he has been?

You may feel that the fear and tension has less of an impact on a modern reader who is used to state-of-the-art technology; but consider the effect on the audience in Stevenson's time. In particular, examine the vocabulary – not just the effect of individual words but the cumulative effect of the vivid descriptions of the supernatural events.

You need to make original points clearly and succinctly and to convince the examiner that your viewpoint is really your own, and a valid one, with constant and careful reference to the text. This will be aided by the use of short and apposite (really relevant) quotations, skilfully embedded in your answer (see 'Sample essays', page 77).

REVIEW YOUR LEARNING

(Answers are given on pp. 102–103.)

1 Will you be assessed on spelling, punctuation and grammar in your response to *Dr Jekyll and Mr Hyde*?

2 Can you take your copy of the novel into the exam?

3 How should you approach the question? What should you do before you embark on the answer?

4 Why is it important to plan your answer?

5 What should you do if you finish ahead of time?

6 Is it enough to refer to the topic in one other place in the novel?

7 Why should you embed quotations?

8 How important is spelling, punctuation and grammar?

9 Are there any ways you can avoid learning quotations?

10 What does 'write in a suitable register' mean?

All GCSE examinations are pinned to specific areas of learning that the examiners want to be sure candidates have mastered. These are known as Assessment Objectives or AOs. If you are studying *Dr Jekyll and Mr Hyde* as an examination text for AQA, Eduqas, OCR or Edexcel, the examiner marking your exam response will be trying to give you marks using the particular mark scheme for that board. The mark schemes for all four boards, however, are based on fulfilling the same key AOs for English literature.

Assessment Objectives

The Assessment Objectives that apply to your response to *Dr Jekyll and Mr Hyde* are shown below.

For all examination boards

AO1 Read, understand and respond to texts. Students should be able to:
- maintain a critical style and develop an informed personal response
- use textual references, including quotations, to support and illustrate interpretations.

AO2 Analyse the language, form and structure used by a writer to create meanings and effects, using relevant subject terminology where appropriate.

For all examination boards except Edexcel

AO3 Show understanding of the relationship between texts and the contexts in which they were written.

If you are entered for the Edexcel examination, AO3 is not assessed on the *Dr Jekyll and Mr Hyde* question; nevertheless the reading and understanding of Chapter 2 'Context' in this guide will increase your understanding and enhance your enjoyment of the novel.

There is one further AO, which applies to OCR only but it is still worth heeding even though it does not apply directly to the other boards.

For OCR only

AO4 Use a range of vocabulary and sentence structures for clarity, purpose and effect, with accurate spelling and punctuation.

You can't forget about AO4 entirely if you are not taking OCR, as it will be assessed on another part of the paper, usually Section A. That being said, if your spelling or punctuation leaves something to be desired you can at least lift your spirits by reminding yourself that AO4 is worth only about 5 per cent of your total mark!

What skills do you need to show?

Let's break down the Assessment Objectives to see what they really mean.

> **AO1** Read, understand and respond to texts. Students should be able to:
> - maintain a critical style and develop an informed personal response
> - use textual references, including quotations, to support and illustrate interpretations.

At its most basic level, this AO is about having a good grasp of what a text is about and being able to express an opinion about it within the context of the question. For example, if you were to say, 'The novel is about a man called Dr Jekyll who can transform himself into Mr Hyde', you would be beginning to address AO1 because you have made a personal response. An 'informed' response refers to the basis on which you make that judgement. In other words, you need to show that you know the novel well enough to answer the question.

AO1 is closely linked to the idea that you are also required to 'use textual references, including quotations, to support and illustrate interpretations.' This means giving short direct quotations from the text. For example, if you wanted to support the idea that Mr Hyde could be violent and aggressive, you could use a direct quote to point to the fact that 'he was trampling his victim under foot'. Alternatively, you can simply refer to details in the text in order to support your views. So you might say, 'Hyde is violent and aggressive because he murders Carew for no apparent reason.' Do make sure, however, that you include some direct quotations to hit this objective, even if they are from the extract itself.

Generally speaking, most candidates find AO1 relatively easy if they have studied the novel and understood it. Usually, it is tackled well. In short, just answer the question you are asked and refer frequently to the key words in that question. Remember, a brief written plan will keep you on track.

> **AO2** Analyse the language, form and structure used by a writer to create meanings and effects, using relevant subject terminology where appropriate.

AO2, however, is a different matter. Most examiners would probably agree that covering AO2 is a weakness for many candidates, particularly for those students who only ever talk about the characters as if they were real people.

In simple terms, AO2 refers to the writer's methods and is often signposted in questions by the word 'how' or the phrase 'How does the writer present…'.

GRADE BOOSTER

Remember: if you do not address AO2 at all, it will be very difficult to achieve much higher than Grade 1, since you will not be answering the question.

Overall AO2 is equal in importance to AO1, so it is vital that you are fully aware of this Assessment Objective. The word 'language' refers to Stevenson's use of words. Remember that writers choose words very carefully in order to achieve particular effects. They may spend quite a long time deciding between two or three words that are similar in meaning in order to create just the precise effect they are looking for.

When you are addressing AO2 in your response to *Dr Jekyll and Mr Hyde*, you will typically find yourself using Stevenson's name and exploring the choices he has made. For example, writing 'Stevenson describes Utterson as "austere"...' will set you on the right path to explaining why this word is an interesting choice. It is this explanation that addresses AO2, whereas 'Utterson was austere with himself' is a simple AO1 comment.

Of course, there is no right or wrong answer but you might write, 'Not only was he rigorously self-disciplined as far as vintage wines were concerned, but sadly he had deprived himself of theatre visits for twenty years even though he enjoyed them. The word austere has a coldness about it but Utterson is also described as "lovable" and as having "an approved tolerance of others". This softens the reader's image of him and helps illustrate the complexities of his character.'

Language encompasses a wide range of writer's methods, such as the use of different types of imagery, words that create sound effects, irony and so on.

AO2 also refers to your use of 'subject terminology'. This means that you should be able to use terms such as 'metaphor', 'alliteration' and 'hyperbole' with confidence and understanding. If you can't remember the term, however, don't despair – you will still gain some marks for explaining the effects being created, but it is easier to write about language features if you can use the technical terms. Remember, even if you do identify language features correctly you won't gain many marks unless you show you are capable of appreciating the effects created by the writer by explaining how they are achieved.

The terms 'form' and 'structure' refer to the kind of text you are studying and how it has been 'put together' by the writer. This might include: the narrative technique used (in *Dr Jekyll and Mr Hyde*, in the first eight chapters, Stevenson uses the third person intrusive narrator); the genre(s) the text is part of; the order of events and the effects created by it; and the way key events are juxtaposed. For example, the description of the dreadful trampling of the small girl in the lonely deserted street in the early hours of the morning follows on from the description of how both Utterson and Enfield endeavour to prevent any interruption to their very enjoyable regular Sunday stroll. It thus offers a powerful contrast and an original introduction to the character of Mr Hyde. Effects of structure can also be seen in the writer's use of sentence lengths and word order (syntax).

> **AO3** Show understanding of the relationship between texts and the contexts in which they were written.

This AO, although not perhaps considered as important as AO1 and AO2, is still worth between 15 and 20 per cent of your total mark in the examination as a whole, and so should not be underestimated. Do remember, however, that it is not assessed for this novel if you are entered with Edexcel.

To cover AO3 you must show that you understand the links between a text and when, why and for whom it was written. For example, some awareness of morality and hypocrisy in Victorian England may well help you to understand Stevenson's' intentions in writing *Dr Jekyll and Mr Hyde*, i.e. to help change the attitudes of a largely middle-class readership. Equally, some knowledge of Stevenson's background might give you useful insight into his attitude towards good and evil and the relationship between science and religion in Victorian England.

You might also consider literary context. *Dr Jekyll and Mr Hyde* was written as a Gothic horror story, of which there is a long tradition beginning with Horace Walpole's 1764 novel *The Castle of Otranto,* which combines fiction, horror and Romanticism. It is important to understand, though, that context should not be just 'bolted on' to your response for no good reason. Remember, you are writing about literature not history, but it is good to show you understand the concerns of the Victorian reader. Knowing something of the context will also enormously increase your enjoyment of the novel.

> **AO4** Use a range of vocabulary and sentence structures for clarity, purpose and effect, with accurate spelling and punctuation.

This AO is fairly self-explanatory but it is worth remembering that it is not assessed in your response to *Dr Jekyll and Mr Hyde* unless you are entered for OCR. A clear and well written response should always be your aim, however, whichever board you are taking. If your spelling is so bad, or your grammar and lack of punctuation so confusing, that the examiner cannot understand what you are trying to express, this will obviously adversely affect your mark.

Similarly, although there are no marks awarded for good handwriting, and none taken away for untidiness or crossings outs, it is obviously important for the examiner to be able easily to read what you have written. If you believe your handwriting is so illegible that it may cause difficulties for the examiner, you need to speak to your school's examination officer in plenty of time before the exam. They may be able to arrange for you to have a scribe or to sit your examination using a word processor.

What you will not gain many marks for

You will **not** gain many marks if you do the following:

- **Retell the story.** You can be sure that the examiner marking your response knows the story inside out. A key feature of the lowest grades is 'retelling the story'. Don't do it.

- **Quote long passages.** Remember, the point is that every reference and piece of quotation must serve a very specific point you are making. If you quote at length, the examiner will have to guess which bit of the quotation you mean to serve your point. Don't impose work on the examiner – be explicit about exactly which words you have found specific meaning in. Keep quotes short and smart.

- **Merely identify literary devices.** You will never gain marks simply for identifying literary devices, such as use of a simile or rhyme. You can gain marks, however, by identifying these features, exploring the reasons you think the author has used them and offering a thoughtful consideration of how they might impact on the reader, as well as giving an evaluation of how effective you think they are.

- **Give unsubstantiated opinions.** The examiner will be keen to give you marks for your opinions, but only if they are supported by reasoned argument and references to the text.

- **Write about characters as if they are real people.** It is important to remember that characters are constructs – the writer is responsible for what the characters do and say. Don't ignore the author!

REVIEW YOUR LEARNING

(Answers are given on p. 103.)

1 What is AO1 assessing?

2 What is AO2 assessing?

3 What is AO3 assessing?

4 What is AO4 assessing?

5 Which exam board specification are you following and what AOs should you be focusing on?

6 What should you *not* do in your responses?

Target your thinking

- What type of question will you face on your GCSE English literature examination?
- What are examiners looking for when they assess your work?
- What are the features of Grade 8 and Grade 5 answers?
- What does a well-structured essay look like?
- What is the most effective way to use quotations and textual references?

Character-based essays

The question below is typical of an AQA question, but is similar to the extract-based question common to all the boards. You are expected to consider the extract (such as this example) and the novel as a whole.

Mr Utterson the lawyer, was a man of rugged countenance that was never lighted by a smile; cold, scanty and embarrassed in discourse; backward in sentiment; lean, long, dusty, dreary and yet somehow lovable. At friendly meetings, and when the wine was to his taste, something eminently human beaconed from his eye; something indeed which never found its way into his talk, but which spoke not only in these silent syllables of the after-dinner face but more often and loudly in the acts of his life. He was austere with himself; drank gin when he was alone, to mortify a taste for vintages; and though he enjoyed the theatre, had not crossed the doors of one for twenty years. But he had an approved tolerance for others; sometimes wondering, almost with envy, at the high-pressure of spirits involved in their misdeeds; and in any extremity inclined to help rather than to reprove. 'I incline to Caine's heresy,' he used to say quaintly: 'I let my brother go to the devil in his own way.' In this character it was frequently his fortune to be the last reputable acquaintance and the last good influence in the lives of down-going men. And to such as these, so long as they came about his chambers, he never marked a shade of change in his demeanour.

No doubt the feat was easy to Mr Utterson; for he was undemonstrative at the best and even his friendship seemed to be founded in a similar catholicity of good nature. It is the mark of a modest man to accept his friendly circle ready made from the hands of opportunity; and that was the lawyer's way. His friends with those of his own blood, or those whom he had known the longest; his affections, like ivy, were the growth of time, they implied no aptness in the object. Hence no doubt the bond that united him to Mr Richard Enfield his distant kinsman, the well-known man about town. It was a nut to crack for many, what these two could see in each other, or what subject they could find in common. It was reported by those who encountered them in their Sunday walks, that they said nothing, looked singularly dull and would hail with obvious relief the appearance of a friend. For all that, the two men put the greatest store by these excursions, counted them the chief jewel of each week, and not only set aside occasions of pleasure but even resisted the calls of business, that they might enjoy them uninterrupted.

Starting with this extract, how does Stevenson present Utterson in *The Strange Case of Dr Jekyll and Mr Hyde*?

Write about:

- how Stevenson presents Utterson in this extract
- how Stevenson presents Utterson in the novel as a whole.

You will see below two exam responses from students working at different levels. They cover much the same points. If you look carefully, however, you will be able to see how Student Y takes similar material to Student X but develops it further, in order to achieve a higher grade.

In addressing the first bullet, both students look at the extract and begin by considering how Utterson's character and appearance are presented in the first paragraph.

Student X, who is likely to achieve a Grade 5, begins the response like this:

I'm going to explain how Stevenson presents Utterson in the extract and then how Stevenson presents Utterson in the novel as a whole. The writer produces a dense descriptive passage on the character which is not integrated into the action or plot of the story. He uses long and involved, complex sentences dividing the phrases with semi-colons and uses heightened vocabulary which was common in 19th century writing. Stevenson uses an interesting sentence to show the subtle kind expressions in Utterson's face when he is relaxed and has had a drink. 'Something eminently human beaconed from his eye...'

In the rest of the paragraph Stevenson lists Utterson's qualities by showing he denies himself pleasures like drinking 'vintages' at home and going to the theatre. Then he makes a joke using quotes from Utterson which refers to Cain killing Abel, to show that Utterson was quaint and to show he knew the Bible. This creates a strong impression. Stevenson then goes on to explain that Utterson was a very humanitarian character, by using euphemism to explain that he was often the last person of good character to influence men who were about to be hanged; 'down-going men'. Utterson did not judge, and did not treat criminals any different from anyone else. This gives the reader the impression that he was not the most exciting person in the world but if you were in trouble he would be a good person to have on your side.

1 There are no marks for this kind of introduction; it's just running down the clock and not leaving time to gain marks for important points.

2 Some examples of writer's methods given but not enough emphasis on the effect Stevenson wished to create.

3 This impression need to be explained.

4 Correct use of terminology.

5 Generalised effects of Stevenson's presentation of Utterson. Comments need to be more precise and tied more closely to the actual text.

Student Y, who is likely to achieve Grade 8, begins like this:

Stevenson's description of Utterson begins with a long sentence suggesting the complexity of his character. He uses adjectival phrases and lists of alliterative adjectives to describe Utterson's dull personality; 'lean, long, dusty, dreary', which at first makes him seen very boring but this is counteracted by the one word at the end of the sentence which is used to great effect. Utterson was 'lovable'!

1 Judicious use of precise reference to support interpretation from the outset.

Stevenson's use of contrast continues to show the different facets of Utterson's character. Although he was austere with himself he did not impose his abstinence upon his friends. Perhaps the absence of vintage wine made Utterson even more appreciative when he supped with friends: 'something eminently human beaconed from his eye' makes him sound like a really kind man and the use of the word 'beaconed' has connotations of a lighthouse shining out to make people feel safe. (RLS came from a long line of lighthouse engineers so he would be familiar with the terminology.)

2 Seamless linking of ideas between paragraphs.

3 Beginning to show some understanding of contextual factors.

Stevenson develops the idea of Utterson's benevolence, by demonstrating his tolerance of criminals and showing he really is a kind old man, who marvels almost enviously at the energy expended in committing crimes rather than condemning the perpetrator.

'I incline towards Caine's heresy...I let my brother go to the devil in his own way.' The Victorian reader would be very familiar with both Old and New Testaments. Through this Biblical allusion and by using irony, Stevenson shows that rather than be like Caine who asked God whether or not he was his brother's keeper, Utterson is very much concerned about his fellow man and this foreshadows the great lengths to which he goes to protect his friend Jekyll in the rest of the novel.

4 Shows understanding of contextual factors.

5 Pointed development and link to the whole novel.

Both students then go on to consider the way that Stevenson describes how Utterson interacts with other people.

Student X continues:

> Stevenson returns to the idea that Utterson is very ordinary and quite unremarkable in the way he makes friends. He doesn't go looking for them he just meets them in the course of his day-to-day living or he is related to them, as is the case with Enfield. They make an unlikely pair but the bond between them is very strong and Stevenson demonstrates this by using the simile, 'his affections, like ivy, were the growth of time.' Ivy is a very strong plant, which grows steadily, year on year. This is true despite them having so little in common and so little to talk about. The writer creates humour by describing how every Sunday, Utterson and Enfield go on a Sunday walk. They seem to have so little in common that they have no conversation, yet both see this walk as being so important, the writer uses the metaphor 'chief jewel' to describe it. The writer emphasises its importance to both of them by letting the reader know that they didn't allow other business or pleasure to prevent their walks. On the other hand the writer does suggest some awkwardness for both of them as they seem very relieved when they meet someone they know as it breaks the silence. This would suggest that there was some tension between them.

1 Clear explanation of the meaning of the simile but could extend a bit further regarding its effect.

2 Sustained focus on the writer.

3 Correct use of subject terminology.

4 Some alternative interpretation – nudging towards Grade 6.

This is a promising start and would suggest that Student X is working at Grade 5 and is demonstrating a 'clear understanding'. The response is well focused on the task and there is clear awareness of Stevenson's methods and their effects on the reader, though these are not always fully explained.

An even better response, however, appears below. Student Y is working at Grade 8. Look carefully and see if you can identify the differences between the two responses.

1 Conceptualised approach – can focus on detail without losing focus of the whole novel as a construct.

In the next paragraph, Stevenson reinforces the ordinariness of Utterson's character and temperament in order to establish his role as the voice of reason in the novel. Utterson's friends come from the people to whom he is related, people he has encountered in his profession and long-standing friends. He takes life as he finds it, but seems particularly fond of Enfield, his young kinsman with whom he takes a walk every Sunday. Stevenson uses gentle humour to describe the relationship between this unlikely pair. As they have so little in common, these excursions tend to be silent affairs where both of them demonstrate some over-enthusiasm when they meet someone they know, as it breaks the silence. Yet on the other hand, these walks are counted as the 'chief jewel' of each week for both of them, the metaphor suggests that it is the one outstanding gem shining out of an otherwise dull social and business calendar which neither of them is willing to forego.

2 Judicious use of vocabulary to describe the effects of the metaphor.

3 Recognises alternative interpretations of characters' actions.

4 Perhaps there could be wider use of subject terminology.

This is clearly at a higher level and is beginning to consider Stevenson's methods in a thoughtful and developed style.

When addressing the presentation of Utterson in the novel as a whole, Student X has this to say:

1 Integrates quotation skilfully.

In the rest of the novel Stevenson goes on to show how caring and concerned Utterson is about Jekyll and how keen he is to protect Jekyll's reputation. He is clearly unhappy about the contents of the will and like Enfield suspects Jekyll is being blackmailed by Hyde. Everything for Utterson has to have an explanation based on reason. The only way Stevenson can make Utterson consider events beyond the normal is through the dream sequence where in a nightmare he encounters Hyde 'with no face' which makes him determined to see him in waking hours so that 'he might see a reason for his friend's strange preference or bondage.' Everything for Utterson has to be based on reason.

2 Shows awareness of the wider context of the writer's intentions in the novel.

As events unfold in the novel, Stevenson presents Utterson as a kind of detective who seeks the help of Lanyon in trying to understand the hold Hyde has over Jekyll while remaining Jekyll's loyal friend. The evidence against Jekyll is mounting. Utterson knows it was Hyde who murdered Carew and he is made aware that Jekyll is lying about the delivery of the letter. Guest points out the similarity between Jekyll's and Hyde's handwriting. At last Utterson realises that Jekyll is 'forging for a murderer.' This is unthinkable, yet Utterson is not prepared to let this interfere with his loyalty to a friend or consider any other explanation. Even when he observes the partial change of Jekyll into Hyde he can only repeat, 'God forgive us.' From then on Utterson maintains his silence despite mounting evidence of the supernatural nature of events. Despite setting up Utterson as a kind of detective, Stevenson maintains Utterson's rigid hold on to reality right up until the end and leaves the reader to make up his own mind what Utterson does once he has read Jekyll's final statement.

3 Further detail needed here to show analysis rather than just observation.

4 Shows clear understanding of the writer's craft.

Again this answer shows some clear, sustained understanding but there is room for improvement. It could be improved by giving some further detail on context, as seen in the next section of Student Y's response.

Student X is showing the ability to achieve Grade 5 with this clear, coherent response. The response never strays from the focus of the question and it is obvious that Student X has a solid grasp of the details of the novel as a whole.

Now look at the way Student Y approaches the presentation of Utterson in the novel as a whole. Throughout the response Student Y sustains a convincing, thoughtful response, which offers a range of interesting interpretations and which covers all the requirements to achieve Grade 8 and possibly higher.

1 Pointed development and link to the whole novel. Notice the slightly tentative style – which may often reflect a sign of a considered response.

2 Critical, exploratory and conceptualised.

> Stevenson reveals most of the events of the novel through Utterson. We learn about the will, the disagreement with Lanyon, the murder of Carew and follow Utterson's reasoned interpretation as Stevenson has established that he is an entirely dependable and trustworthy character, or so it would seem. He is a character so full of contradictions. He is a lawyer, but has little to say; he likes fine wine and theatre but has denied himself any sensual pleasures. His friends seem self-obsessed and he seems to gain nothing from friendships except some satisfaction of living vicariously through others and filling his time. He has a very rigid view of the world and reality and cannot consider alternative explanations. He is very patient and keeps returning to Jekyll's house despite being turned away by Poole. In short, Stevenson has created a stubborn character who clings to one view of the world, and even when faced with irrefutable evidence will not accept that supernatural events are taking place before his very eyes.
>
> His one action which is proactive and appears out of character is when he goes in search of Hyde. This is precipitated by his nightmare, the only way it seems that Stevenson can introduce any awareness of events beyond what is natural. Utterson is clearly

3 Original interpretation evident from the one excellent choice of word – 'teases'.

4 The student's judicious choice of the word 'just' gives a sense of appreciation of anticlimax.

> disturbed by Enfield's story and it has affected his subconscious. He is always looking for a rational explanation of events which grow weaker as the novel progresses or he goes completely silent. When he and Enfield glimpse the beginning of the change of Jekyll into Hyde in the Incident at the Window, when Stevenson teases the reader by making him think that Utterson is finally going to accept that something completely out of the realms of normality is taking place. He and Enfield look at each other 'with answering horror in their eyes.' Utterson repeats 'God forgive us!' But then, they just return home in silence.

This response is convincing and there are signs of an exploratory approach and analysis of Stevenson's methods. There is judicious use of precise reference to support interpretations. An essay continuing along these lines would certainly be achieving at the highest level.

Theme-based essays

The following sample responses are based on an extract question that focuses on theme rather than character. The format for the question is as for Edexcel but it is similar to one that might be set by any of the four examination boards (remember, for Edexcel no marks are awarded for addressing context but for other boards it is a requirement). Overall the distribution of marks varies for all the boards but the Assessment Objectives remain the same. Responses to AQA, OCR and Eduqas questions are marked holistically but responses to Edexcel questions are separated into two sections, each out of twenty marks.

'Sir,' said I, affecting a coolness that I was far from truly possessing, 'you speak enigmas, and, you will perhaps not wonder that I hear you with no very strong impression of belief. But I have gone too far in the way of inexplicable services to pause before I see the end.'

'It is well,' replied my visitor. 'Lanyon, you remember your vows: what follows is under the seal of our profession. And now, you have so long been bound to the most narrow and material views, you have denied the virtue of transcendental medicine, you have derided your superiors – behold!'

He put the glass to his lips, and drank at one gulp. A cry followed; he reeled, staggered, clutched at the table and held on, staring with infected eyes, gasping with open mouth; and as I looked, there came, I thought, a change – he seemed to swell – his face became suddenly black, and the features seem to melt and alter – and the next moment I had sprung to my feet and leaped back against the wall, my arm raised to shield me from that prodigy, my mind submerged into terror.

'Oh God!' I screamed, and 'O God!' again and again; for there before my eyes – pale and shaken, and half fainting and groping before me with his hands, like a man restored from death – Henry Jekyll!

What he told me in the next hour I cannot bring myself to set on paper. I saw what I saw, I heard what I heard, and my soul sickened at it; and yet, now when the sight has faded from my eyes, I ask myself if I believe it, and I cannot answer. My life is shaken to its roots; sleep has left me; the deadliest terror sits by me at all hours of the day and night; I feel that my days are numbered, and that I must die; and yet I shall die incredulous. As for the moral turpitude that man unveiled to me, even with tears of penitence, I cannot, even in memory, dwell on it without a start of horror. I will say but one thing, Utterson, and that (if you can bring your mind to credit it) will be more than enough. The creature who crept into my house that night was, on Jekyll's own confession, known by the name of Hyde and hunted for in every corner of the land as the murderer of Carew.

Hastie Lanyon

Explore how Stevenson presents horror in this extract taken from 'Dr Lanyon's Narrative'.

Give examples from the extract to support your ideas. (20 marks)

In this extract a strong sense of horror is created.

Explain why horror is important elsewhere in the novel.

In your answer you must consider:

- how Stevenson creates an atmosphere of horror
- how it appeals to the emotional rather than the rational side of human nature. (20 marks)

Student X, who is hoping to achieve a Grade 5, begins like this:

1 How?

> Horror is an important theme in Dr Jekyll and Mr Hyde and as part of the Gothic novel is meant to make the reader experience deep fear which cannot be explained in terms of nature. In the extract, the visitor, who has come to Lanyon for the chemicals in the drawer, has given Lanyon the choice of whether to stay and watch what happens next. Stevenson makes Lanyon's discomfort clear from the start of the extract: 'affecting a coolness I was far from truly possessing' is an understatement yet Lanyon has decided he has become too involved just to walk away. Here Stevenson uses dramatic irony because the reader already knows that the visitor is Hyde but Lanyon doesn't and this adds to the horror.

> Hyde's reply is very theatrical, which is unusual as he usually talks in grunts and monosyllables. Here Stevenson makes him speak in a very flamboyant way using long words and sentences, finally ending with the one word sentence ending with an exclamation mark, 'Behold!' This sounds like a stage magician to a modern reader but to Victorians it would be horrific.

2 Why?

3 Use of subject terminology.

> In the next paragraph Stevenson describes the physical change in the visitor by using lists of very expressive verbs, such as 'reeled', 'staggered', 'clutched', 'gasping', which build up the horror and it reaches a climax when Lanyon jumps back and hits the wall and describes his 'mind submerged in terror.' This is very effective as the word 'submerged' makes it sound like he is drowning in terror.

4 More development of explanation of effects needed to move answer to Grade 6, though the comment on drowning is a move in that direction.

> The sense of horror reaches a terrifying climax in the next paragraph. Stevenson expresses the horror and Lanyon's terror on one long sentence broken up by commas, semi-colons and dashes. Lanyon screams out 'O God!' and repeats it over and over. To a Victorian audience who has not experienced

5 Comment on context neatly integrated although will not be assessed for Edexcel.

the effects created by modern technology this would be very horrific and the use of the word God in those days would be taken very seriously because one of the Ten Commandments is you shouldn't use the word God in normal conversation unless you really mean it. Clearly a supernatural event is taking place. This is the scene of the book which modern horror films concentrate on as it is the most effective. Stevenson's use of dialogue shows how hysterical Lanyon is which adds to the horror of the scene.

6 This paragraph shows understanding of the techniques the writer is using to create horror and commenting on their effectiveness. The answer is moving steadily towards a Grade 6.

Student X writes about the final paragraph in the extract at much the same level and then moves on to the second part of the question.

Another place in the novel where Stevenson creates a strong sense of horror is in the very short chapter 'Incident at the Window.' This chapter illustrates 'calm before the storm' as the reader is lulled into a false sense of security. Utterson and Enfield are amiably strolling in front of Jekyll's residence on another Sunday afternoon when they remember events that took place there and with some gentle rebuke Enfield lets Utterson know he has since realised he had been tricked into disclosing Jekyll's identity. However they both show relief that the whole Hyde episode is over.

Stevenson uses pathetic fallacy by describing the weather in the lead up to them seeing a sickly looking Jekyll at the window. The light is changing and the courtyard is in twilight but overhead the sun is still shining. Jekyll appears pleased to see them and Utterson introduces his kinsman. Stevenson maintains the atmosphere of calm by continuing a dialogue of pleasant conversation through the open window about nothing in particular. Jekyll smiles and then suddenly... everything changes, starting with his face. A look

1 Apt choice – short and manageable episode.

2 Clear, explained response.

3 Correct use of subject terminology, which shows understanding of writer's methods, but more explanation of the effects is needed.

of 'abject terror and despair' comes over it and it is contorted. Utterson and Enfield see enough for it to freeze their blood before Jekyll slams the window shut. This is the point in the novel where the reader cannot doubt that something really abnormal is happening as Utterson and Enfield are so terrified of the horror of the situation. They have horror in their eyes. Utterson says a prayer like it is necessary to ward off evil spirits and then they just walk off in silence. On that note the chapter ends, leaving the reader on a high.

4 Quotations again skilfully integrated.

5 Attempts to explain the effect on the reader but style is overly colloquial.

Overall Student X clearly fulfils the criteria for Grade 5 and in places edges towards a Grade 6. The answer shows clear understanding of the text. It is sustained and consistent in quality and includes clear explanations of the writer's methods and some of the effects using subject terminology. The overall general descriptor of a Grade 5 answer is that it shows clear understanding of the ideas, perspectives and context of the novel.

The following is a partial answer in response to the second half of the question written by Student Y, who is expected to achieve a Grade 8 or even higher.

1 Analysis of writer's methods – uses subject terminology judiciously.

There are two other significant episodes in the novel where horror is most evident: the murder of Carew and the incident at the window.

Stevenson presents the first incident from the perspective of a maid dreaming of romance and watching the moon from her bedroom on a clearly lit evening. This use of pathetic fallacy is typical of the foreshadowing of events in Gothic horror. The moon, the fog rolling off the river and the love-struck maiden are all ingredients to be found in this genre. After witnessing the horrific attack on the kindly old man with white hair, this damsel in distress typically faints (fainting females are a common feature of Gothic horror).

What is even more horrific for the reader is the description of the uncontrolled violence. This has a

2 Clear analysis of how the tale fits the genre.

3 Clear analysis of language techniques.

4 Clear analysis of the effects of the language used.

great emotional impact on the reader as Stevenson has already established Carew's benign credentials by using adjectives such as 'pretty manner of politeness' and 'an innocent and old-world kindness of disposition.' Contrast this with the writer's use of the simile — Hyde's 'ape-like fury' and the audible shattering of bones as he jumps on the kindly old man sickens the reader to his very core. The effect is horrific. The use of the visual and auditory senses makes it so. The violence of the verbs 'was trampling', 'hailing down' and 'shattered' gives the reader the feeling that the violence and the horror was relentless and the only option for the young maid was to faint. The suddenness of this episode also adds to the horror, Stevenson likens it to 'a flame of anger' which surprised the old gentleman and the maid later describes them as being the actions of a madman.

5 Critical and exploratory conceptualised response to 'elsewhere in the text'.

The examiner comments are as follows:

The whole of this section shows an insightful analysis of language supported by a judicious use of subject terminology. (AQA)

The response is a cohesive evaluation of the interrelationship of language and its effect on the reader. (Edexcel)

Textual references and quotations are precise, pertinent and interwoven. There is detailed and well-developed analysis of the writer's use of language, form and structure to create meanings and effects. (OCR)

Overall, Student Y has produced a considered and thoughtful response with impressive detailed support and some interesting interpretations and deeper meanings. He or she has demonstrated an ability to unpick small parts of the text to show a comprehensive appreciation of Stevenson's methods.

As your examination will be 'closed book' and you will have only a short extract in front of you, you might find it helpful to memorise some quotations to use in support of your points in the examination response, particularly when addressing the question with regard to the rest of the novel (please see the 'Tackling the exams' section on page 59 for further information about the format of the examination).

please see the 'Tackling the exams' section on page 59 for further information about the format of the examination

> **GRADE** *BOOSTER*
>
> It will help you in the exam if you select ten quotations to learn, or at least paraphrase, from across the sections below. This will boost your confidence and help you organise your thoughts when planning your answer.
>
> You don't need to remember long quotations; short quotes that you can embed into a sentence will be far more effective. If all else fails, as long as you can remember the gist of what the quotation relates to, you can use a textual reference.

All four exam boards have an extract-based question and this is designed to help you use quotations, so if your memory fails you can select apt words or phrases from the passage as this will fulfil the part of AO1 relating to quoting from the text, and then just make textual references to other places in the novel. Remember, the examiner is looking for an individual, conceptualised, analytical response to the novel and is not really testing your ability to learn long passages parrot-fashion.

Top ten characterisation quotations

The following quotations can be used as a quick reminder of the way that Stevenson has presented the key characteristics of each of the main characters.

Utterson

'Cold, scanty and embarrassed in discourse; backward in sentiment; lean, long, dusty, dreary and yet somehow lovable.'

1

- Reveals the contradictions within Utterson's personality.

GRADE *BOOSTER*

As evidence of Utterson's nature, you could use the full first quotation, but you could also say that unusually for a lawyer, Utterson appeared silent and aloof and a dull character, yet people found him 'lovable'.

2 'He was austere with himself; drank gin when he was alone to mortify a taste for vintages.'

- Reveals remarkable self-control and self-denial, characteristically old-fashioned Christian virtues upheld by Victorian society.

GRADE *BOOSTER*

The most often used method for learning quotations is to write them down, repeat them and then test yourself. If you are a visual learner, however, you might try capturing one of these quotes in a drawing with the quotation as a caption.

Edward Hyde

3 'Mr Hyde was pale and dwarfish, he gave the impression of deformity without any nameable malformation.'

- Each character who encounters Hyde is aware of there being an abnormality about Hyde without being able to say what it is. The metaphor comparing him to a dwarf suggests that his growth was stunted by evil.

Henry Jekyll

4 '...a large, well-made, smooth-faced man of fifty, with something of a slyish cast perhaps'

- Stevenson's physical description of Jekyll suggests from the outset that there is an element of secrecy about the protagonist and that there is a side to his personality that is not immediately apparent.

5 'It was thus rather the exacting nature of my aspirations, rather than any particular degradation in my faults, that made me what I was.'

- Jekyll's rather arrogant view of his own character.

Lanyon

'...an excellent fellow, and I always mean to see more of him: but a hide-bound pedant for all that; an ignorant, blatant pedant.'

6

- Jekyll's view of Lanyon, yet it is to him that he turns when he is in trouble.

'As for the moral turpitude that man unveiled to me... I cannot, even in memory, dwell on it without a start of horror.'

7

- On seeing Hyde transform into Jekyll, and having come face to face with pure evil, Lanyon can no longer cope with this knowledge and goes into a terminal decline.

Enfield

Utterson's 'distant kinsman, the well-known man about town.'

8

- Enfield's main role in the novel is to introduce Hyde and to recount the first of his atrocities: the mowing down of the small girl.

'I am ashamed of my long tongue. Let us make a bargain never to refer to this again.'

9

- Enfield genuinely has a distaste for gossip and feels that he has been tricked by Utterson into revealing information about Henry Jekyll.

Poole

'"The doctor was confined to the house," Poole said, "and saw no-one."'

10

- Poole's role in the novel is to facilitate the action. Prior to Chapter 8 'The Last Night', it has consisted largely of turning away visitors. In this chapter, however, he plays a large part as he becomes **everyman**. Poole is the character who puts his thoughts and fears into terms that the reader can interpret as supernatural events.

Everyman: a literary term that has come to mean an ordinary person with whom the reader identifies and whose experiences he shares in peculiar circumstances.

Top ten moments in the novel

1 '...the man trampled calmly over the child's body and left her screaming on the ground.'

- The trampling of the small girl is a key moment because the reader is first made aware of the evil character, Hyde.

2 'The fact is, if I do not ask you the name of the other party, it is because I know it already.'

- Utterson recognising whose house the door belongs to is key as it establishes the connection between Jekyll and Hyde.

GRADE *BOOSTER*

The memory part of your brain loves colour! Try copying these quotations using different colours for different characters. You might organise them into mind maps, or write them on to sticky notes and put them up around your room. Flash cards can also be fun and effective if you can enlist the help of a partner.

3 'If he be Mr Hyde... I shall be Mr Seek'

- Utterson hunting down Hyde is a key moment as it establishes Utterson's devotion and loyalty and his determination to protect the reputation of his friend Jekyll.

4 'This is a matter I had thought we had agreed to drop.'

- Utterson visits Jekyll, who refuses to discuss the fact that he has made Hyde the sole beneficiary of his will. This is key in establishing the sense of mystery.

5 'The murderer was gone long ago; but there lay his victim in the middle of the lane, incredibly mangled.'

- The murder of Carew. This action is key as it is what ultimately brings about the downfall of Jekyll.

6 'Mr Hyde had disappeared out of the ken of the police as though he had never existed.'

- Hyde disappears. His disappearance is key as it allows Stevenson to re-establish the relationship between the three friends.

'But it bore no postmark. The note was handed in.'

7

- Jekyll lies about the letter. This moment is key because Utterson has to face the fact that Jekyll is lying to him.

'A week afterwards Dr Lanyon took to his bed, and in something less than a fortnight he was dead.'

8

- Lanyon's sudden deterioration, followed by his death. This moment is key as it confirms that supernatural forces are at work. Lanyon has recognised the duality of his own nature and recognised the evil within himself.

'...an expression of such abject terror and despair as froze the very blood of the two gentlemen below.'

9

- Jekyll's spontaneous transformation at the window. This moment is key because Enfield and Utterson are faced with irrefutable evidence of supernatural activity.

'"We have come too late," he [Utterson] said sternly, "whether to save or punish."'

10

- Poole and Utterson break into the laboratory at the moment Jekyll commits suicide. This brings the action of the novel to its conclusion.

Top ten thematic quotations

The duality of human nature

'I learned to recognise the thorough and primitive duality of man; I saw that of the two natures that contended in the field of my consciousness, even if I could rightly be said to be either, it was only because I was radically both.'

1

- Jekyll explains that after taking the drug, Hyde is the embodiment of his (Jekyll's) evil side, yet Jekyll himself is unchanged. Evil and goodness still exist within him but his evil side is generally controlled by his conscience, what Freud called the superego.

Stevenson describes Hyde as having 'Satan's signature upon his face'.

2

- Exemplifies how Stevenson uses language features such as metaphor and alliteration to establish the presence of evil from the very first encounter between Utterson and Hyde.

> **GRADE BOOSTER**
>
> ```
> Another useful method is to record quotations and play
> them over and over. Or you might try watching one of
> the many adaptations to spot where a quote appears.
> This can be an effective method as you have both sound
> and vision to help you, and you can see the quotations
> in context.
> ```

3 '...that man is not truly one, but truly two. I say two because my own knowledge does not pass beyond that point.'

- Jekyll on his own 'scientific' discovery.

Hypocrisy and respectability

4 'Though so profound a double-dealer, I was in no sense a hypocrite...'

- The reader may profoundly disagree with Jekyll's view of himself for several reasons, not least because he enjoys the evil side of his nature but fails to admit that it is just as much part of his character as is the respectable doctor, much loved by his servants.

Silence and secrecy

5 'Utterson... this is a private matter, and I beg you to let it sleep.'

- Jekyll, regarding the contents of his will.

6 'Five minutes afterwards, if you insist upon an explanation, you will have understood that these arrangements are of capital importance'

- From Jekyll's written instructions to Lanyon regarding the procurement of the potion.

Rationalism and the supernatural

7 'Your master, Poole, is plainly seized with one of those maladies that both torture and deform the sufferer. ... There is my explanation; it is sad enough, Poole, ay and appalling to consider; but it is plain and natural, hangs well together and delivers us from all exorbitant alarms.'

- Utterson's feeble attempt to rationalise the strange happenings in the locked laboratory.

'…the hair stood upon my head like quills. Sir, if that was my master, why had he a mask upon his face?'

8

- Poole's response to Utterson about the same supernatural Jekyll/Hyde presence in the locked laboratory.

The beast in man

'…with ape-like fury, he was trampling his victim under foot, and hailing a storm of blows, under which bones were audibly shattered and the body jumped upon the roadway.'

9

- Stevenson's description of the murder of Carew. Note the vivid verbs and the onomatopoeic quality of 'audibly shattered'. The words are specially chosen to sicken the reader. This quotation exemplifies how bestial and completely out of control Hyde is, that he attacks a defenceless old man without any provocation.

Violence

'And then came the horrible part of the thing; for the man trampled calmly over the child's body and left her screaming on the ground.'

10

- Enfield's use of the word 'calmly' ironically emphasises the viciousness of the act. The juxtaposition of the words 'man' and 'child' highlight the abomination of the careless abuse.

Works of fiction by Robert Louis Stevenson

- *Treasure Island* (1883)
- *Prince Otto* (1885)
- *Kidnapped* (1886)
- *The Black Arrow: A Tale of the Two Roses* (1888)
- *The Master of Ballantrae* (1888)

Critical interpretation

- Masao Miyoshi (1969) *The Divided Self*

Useful websites and online resources

- www.aqa.org.uk
- http://qualifications.pearson.com
- www.ocr.org.uk
- www.eduqas.co.uk
- https://en.wikipedia.org
- http://robertlouisstevenson.co.uk
- http://robert-louis-stevenson.org
- www.biography.com/people/robert-louis-stevenson-9494571
- www.online-literature.com/stevenson
- www.learnlibrary.com/jekyll-hyde/jekyll-hyde_1.htm (free online ebook)
- http://etc.usf.edu/lit2go (download the audiobook on to your tablet or mp3 player)
- https://itunes.apple.com/gb/course/strange-case-dr.-jekyll-mr./id654432827 (BLIS–Bilkent University free online course for iGCSE English literature: *Strange Case of Dr Jekyll and Mr Hyde*, useful to guide you through the first reading of the novel)
- www.youtube.com (free audio plus fascinating videos)
- www.bl.uk (the British Library website, see the article 'Discovering literature: Romantics and Victorians')

Well-known nineteenth-century Gothic novels

- Jane Austen (1818) *Northanger Abbey*
- Charlotte Brontë (1847) *Jane Eyre*
- Emily Brontë (1847) *Wuthering Heights*

- Charles Dickens (1861) *Great Expectations*
- Henry James (1898) *The Turn of the Screw*
- Victor Hugo (1831) *The Hunchback of Notre-Dame*
- Edgar Allan Poe (1849) *Tales of Mystery and Imagination*
- Mary Shelley (1818) *Frankenstein*
- Bram Stoker (1897) *Dracula*
- Oscar Wilde (1890) *The Picture of Dorian Gray*

Popular modern Gothic novels

- Virginia Andrews (1979) *Flowers in the Attic*
- Dan Brown (2003) *The Da Vinci Code*
- Tracy Chevalier (1999) *The Girl with the Pearl Earring*
- Douglas Clegg (2006) *Isis*
- Susan Hill (1983) *The Woman in Black*
- Stephen King (1977) *The Shining*
- Stephanie Meyer (2005) the *Twilight* series
- Patrick Suskind (1985) *Perfume: The Story of a Murderer*
- Donna Tart (1992) *The Secret History*
- Sarah Waters (2009) *The Little Stranger*

Answers to the 'Review your learning' sections.

Context (p. 18)

1   A lung disease.
2   Context: existing knowledge, beliefs, the scientific advances, historical and political circumstances of the time.
3   Financial independence.
4   Science vs religion; human responsibility; good vs evil; drug taking.
5   To appeal to a wider readership.
6   Presbyterianism preaches strict adherence to the Ten Commandments. A bohemian lifestyle is much more free and relaxed.
7   The Gothic novel is written to frighten, to thrill and terrify the reader.
8   Laudanum was a solution of opium drugs in alcohol.
9   Stevenson rejected Christianity and his family for a time.
10 Not to draw definite conclusions that anything in this novel is autobiographical, but to raise ideas as possibilities.

Plot and structure (p. 29)

1   Jekyll wrote the £100 compensation cheque that Hyde gave to the girl's family. Hyde is the sole beneficiary in Jekyll's will.
2   'Sawbones' – the Edinburgh doctor was 'as emotional as a bagpipe'.
3   He dreams of Hyde trampling the small girl, just as Enfield recounted.
4   Jekyll's original will states that, should he die or disappear, Edward Hyde should be his sole heir.
5   Jekyll calls Lanyon 'an ignorant, blatant pedant' because Lanyon has called Jekyll's scientific work heresies.
6   'She had an evil face smoothed by hypocrisy but her manners were excellent.' The contrast between her appearance and her behaviour adds depth to her character and may make the reader think she is an ideal caretaker for a character like Hyde, as she too can adapt and change in response to circumstances almost seamlessly.
7   Lanyon dies because he recognises the evil within himself; he cannot come to terms with this knowledge.
8   Poole heard his master cry out 'upon the name of God' and since then he has not heard his voice but the voice of an imposter.
9   Dr Jekyll. He meant that he paid the price for his curiosity.
10 He felt it was his duty to help an old friend; however he agreed partly out of curiosity.

Characterisation (p. 39)

1   They can't describe him but they felt that he was deformed in some way.

2   Mr Guest, Utterson's clerk.

3   Utterson. It is a handicap as speaking is the main skill of a lawyer.

4   They are both proud doctors. Stevenson uses both to exemplify the duality of human nature.

5   Hyde is likened to a snake, a rat and an ape.

6   Jekyll revelled in his guilty pleasures and did not accept any responsibility for Hyde's actions.

7   Almost all of the male characters are rich, successful, middle-class professionals; the adult female characters are all servants.

8   Richard Enfield; his main role is to introduce Edward Hyde.

9   The maid at the window is a stereotype of the Gothic novel because she faints at the sight of Hyde's unbridled attack on Carew.

10 Dr Denman was the previous owner of Jekyll's residence and laboratory.

Themes (p. 51)

1   A theme is a central idea that a writer explores through the plot, structure, characters and descriptions in a novel.

2   A motif is an idea or object that recurs throughout a literary work.

3   The main themes in the novel are: the duality of human nature; secrecy, hypocrisy; the supernatural; violence and repression.

4   Stevenson was interested in exploring the human condition and the nature of good and evil.

5   '…with ape-like fury, he was trampling his victim underfoot' exemplifies both the beast in man and Hyde's 'troglodytic' behaviour.

6   Utterson represents rationalism; Jekyll/Hyde represents the supernatural.

7   Stevenson creates the atmosphere of secrecy by withholding information.

8   Doors, windows, mirrors, masks, light and dark are the main motifs introduced by Stevenson into the novel.

9   The back door is discoloured, blistered, no bell or knocker. The front door, in contrast, 'wore a great air of wealth and comfort' and had both a knocker and a fanlight.

10 Light and darkness symbolise good and evil and are used to create an atmosphere of secrecy, tension and foreboding.

Language, style and analysis (p. 58)

1 The term 'form' refers to the choices that the writer makes in terms of how he tells the story, or in other words, the viewpoint.

2 Use of the third person allows the writer both to narrate events and to comment on them.

3 Alliteration means using words close to each other that begin with the same sound to create effect.

4 Simile and metaphor.

5 The term 'pathetic fallacy' was coined by Ruskin for when settings, particularly the weather, are described by giving them human qualities.

6 A symbol is an object that represents other things of a wider importance, for instance light and darkness.

7 The language of working-class people is less elaborate; their speech is ungrammatical; their vocabulary is comparatively limited.

8 Many possible answers (ask your teacher to check your answer).

9 When Hyde confronts Lanyon just before he changes back to Jekyll, he launches into an elaborate, stylish speech of triumph (more like Jekyll).

10 To show off your analytical skills and to show a deeper understanding of the author's choices.

Tackling the exams (p. 71)

1 No, **or** Yes, as I am sitting the OCR exam.

2 No.

3 Read the extract carefully. Think about the focus of the question. Underline key words. Make a plan. Sort your ideas in number order.

4 To keep focused on the question; to give a framework to express ideas logically and in sequence; to make sure all the Assessment Objectives are addressed.

5 Check your answer carefully:

- Make sure it is clear.
- Make sure you have shown understanding and interpretation of the novel and have focused on the question.
- Check you have written about Stevenson and how he has used language, structure and form.
- Check for awareness of context (**not** Edexcel candidates).
- Check you have included quotations (preferably embedded) to support your points.
- Rectify any omissions/errors.
- Check your vocabulary and sentence constructions. Check spelling and punctuation (for OCR).

6   While generally the maxim is to write a lot about a little, for AQA and Eduqas you **must** refer to the **whole** novel.

7   It is important to make the individual quotations you select brief and to try to embed them. This saves time, and you can cover more points.

8   It is not specifically important, except for OCR (4 marks). **But** you cannot express yourself effectively without accurate punctuation and grammar.

9   You can use apt quotations from the extract to meet the Assessment Objectives, but it is advisable to learn some very short quotations (see the 'Top ten' section, page 91, for advice).

10 'Write in a suitable register' means to adopt a formal academic style: don't use colloquial language; refer to the writer by surname; suggest rather that state interpretations.

Assessment Objectives and skills (p. 76)

1   AO1 is assessing textual knowledge and understanding, personal response and the ability to back up points with quotations and close references to the text.

2   AO2 is assessing ability to write about language, form and structure, i.e. the writer's craft.

3   AO3 is understanding context.

4   AO4 is using vocabulary and sentence structures for clarity, purpose and effect; accurate spelling and punctuation.

5   For AQA: AO1, AO2 and AO3.
    For OCR: AO1, AO2, AO3 and AO4.
    For Edexcel: AO1 and AO2.
    For Eduqas: AO1, AO2 and AO3.

6   Do **not**: retell the story, quote at length, simply identify devices without explaining their effects, offer unsupported opinions, or write about characters as if they were real people. Keep referring to the writer to stay focused on the question.